How To Make Money Make Sense To Children

by
Michael J. Searls

Summit Financial Publishing books are available at
special discounts for bulk pruchases, for sales promotions, fund raising or educational purchases. Special
editions can be created to specifications. For details,
contact: Special Sales Department, Summit Financial
Publishing, 19590 E. Main St., ste. 108, Parker, CO
80134.

Library of Congress Cataloging-in-Publication Data

Contents

PART III
Applying the Money Management System

Introduction

But First, A Word from Our Sponsor

Business is more instinctive with kids than most parents realize. At lunch time in any school you'll hear: Bartering: "I'll trade my banana for your sandwich." Negotiation: "Okay, if you'll give me a swizzle licorice, too." Marketing: "My mom makes the absolute best cookies; you'll love them."

Regardless of what your children know about economics, and whether or not you have taught them financial responsibility, kids practice business each and every day, even if they don't know they're doing it. In the cafeteria, some kids are selling t-shirts to raise money for the school band; someone is passing out fliers and talking up the Halloween dance in the gym. There are kids swapping baseball cards and sharing leads on baby sitting jobs. Two others, having become partners, are targeting potential yard work customers. And everyone is talking about ways to spend money: hot sneakers and team jackets, computer games and videos, snowboards and roller blades, fast food and movies.

And today's world of kids and money is not nickel and dime. Far from it. The 29 million American adolescents take in an astounding $102 billion (yes, that's billion) a year from jobs, allowance, cash gifts, savings bonds, and other investments. These same teens spend $67 billion annually and, by directing their parents toward certain products, influence the household spending of another $42 billion. This influence includes the household expenditures on everything from cold cereal and movies to the choice of family dining and vacation destinations.

Even kids ages four to 12 have enormous financial clout. The 35 million members of this age group had a recent total annual income of $20.3 billion and spent $17.1 billion of it according to James McNeal, a marketing professor at Texas A&M University. McNeal figures that these younger kids directly influence about $170 billion in family spending. As the late Senator from Illinois, Everett Dirksen, reportedly observed, "A billion here, a billion there, and pretty soon you're talking big money."

Kids are handling money, and lots of it, yet few children or adolescents really know how to handle it properly. How may kids have a clue about how much their parents earn? Or how much the house or car cost? Many parents avoid teaching their offspring the principles of economics and smart money management. In numerous households, "money" is a dirty word, never to be discussed in public and certainly never in front of the children. "Money is the root of all evil," goes the familiar saying. (Which, by the way, is a misquotation. The original Biblical passage in I Timothy 6:10 says, "The adoration of money is the root of all evil.")

Our children are learning life skills now regardless of whether we're the ones teaching them or not. Perhaps they are learning not to care about money, or to fear it, or feel guilty about it, or to be greedy. Whatever the lesson, they are probably modeling whatever they see their parents doing. As in other areas of life, children learn financial behavior by watching what their parents do. Even sadder than how financially ignorant most children and young adults are is how financially ignorant their parents are.

We grown-ups sit down to make a household spending budget, only to disregard it when we want something we really can't afford. Not many of us are putting away a set amount every week or month for the kids' college and for our own retirement. And then there are those of us who raid our savings from time to time when the credit card bill is higher than our checking account balance.

Granted, many American parents have no choice but to live from paycheck to paycheck. Wouldn't it be nice, though, if our children never have to do that because the principles of money management are instilled at an early age.

Will teaching kids about money make them greedy? No, I don't think so. For many years, I was an investment consultant, working with a number of clients and many millions of dollars. I bring this up only to relate an observation: The really successful people tell me that they were taught how to handle money wisely from an early age; those people who simply inherited a lot of money without first being properly prepared often watched helplessly as their fortune dwindled away.

Eighty-five percent of what we know about money is taught to us by our parents. Yet most parents say they don't know enough about money. If this is the case, why not adopt a system that focuses on principles and not on the guilt or greed. Let's give our kids a method by which they can manage their money today in a way that makes sense, one that will provide a life skill which they can practice for the rest of their lives. The Four-Part Money Management System is just such a method.

Many parents say, "My kindergartner is too young to handle money. We give her a dollar and she immediately loses it."

Yet, psychologist Ray Guarendi told *Working Mother* that age six is a good time to introduce a regular allowance. "This is the best tool for teaching kids to be smart money managers. It gives them first-hand experience budgeting, saving, and making spending decisions."

Financial educator Janet Bodnar, writing in *Parents*, agrees that " . . . Between the ages of seven and ten, children develop a grasp of the abstract notion we call money."

Even if parents choose to keep their kids ignorant about the world of money, American companies recognize that very young children have enormous financial clout. Think of the advertising, promotions and products specifically geared to the preschool set. Everyone knows that Saturday morning network TV has almost as many commercials selling cold cereal, candy, and toys, as it has cartoons. Because of this, many people insist that their children watch only public TV, so their kids aren't "polluted" by consumerism. Fine, but ask your preschoolers what the hottest toys are: Beany Babies? Tickle Me Elmos? Barney dolls? Sesame Street characters? Even public television is capitalizing on consumerism.

It's never too early for a child to start learning about the world of finance. Certainly by the time a kid becomes a teenager, if financial discipline is not part of her or his makeup, it may be too late. No responsible parent would send a teenager out in the world without an understanding about drugs, sex, drinking, and driving. Why would that same parent ignore rearing financially responsible, financially smart kids? If kids see only the unwise management of money growing up, then those lessons may stay with them forever.

Teaching kids about money is a crucial parenting responsibility, and it can even be fun. Kids delight in learning. Kids enjoy pleasing their parents. And parents glow when their kids master new information and skills. And who knows, maybe along the way we grown-ups will pick up a pointer or two.

Teaching kids about money can bring out the best — and the worst — in you. Young children may be slow to grasp certain financial concepts or be resistant to change in the domestic status quo. Older kids, used to getting what they want, may view your help as parental intrusion or boring or a waste of time. And opening yourself up to kids' questions and criticism about your own financial habits may push all sorts of emotional buttons. As the famous economist John Kenneth Galbraith observed in *The Age of Uncertainty*, "Money is a singular thing. It ranks with love as man's greatest source of joy. And with death as his greatest source of anxiety."

The important thing is to keep your sense of humor and to remember that you're teaching your kids something they can learn well only from you.

Part I of *How To Make Money Make Sense To Children* provides an historical, social, and cultural context for the evolution of money and economics and offers perspective for the importance of understanding these concepts in today's economy.

Part II focuses on the teaching aspects and provides background and a framework for parents to teach their kids about money management.

Part III presents the Four-Part Money Management System, which is based on the simple principles of spend, give, save and invest. This system works whether you're five years old, 15 years old, or 55 years young. The chapters in this section show parents how to instill these principles and other important financial information in children of various ages.

At the end of each chapter is a list of resources — books, web sites, organizations, financial institutions, etc. — you can turn to for more information.

Like other lessons in life, learning about money should be serious business. But it can also be entertaining and informative, which is what *How To Make Money Make Sense To Children* strives to be. After all, what could be better than laughing all the way to the bank!

Part I

Money Makes
The World Go Round

Chapter 1

When I Was Your Age . . .

Not long ago, my 12-year-old daughter came to me and asked for $10. Mindful that I had given her $10 just the day before, I asked her what she had done with it. "I lost it," she replied — somewhat indifferently, I thought.

The incident stuck in my mind and haunted me like a final-but-missing piece of a puzzle I knew by heart. After all, she's a wonderful young woman with loads of promise and potential and, I like to think, has been raised well by her caring and very smart parents.

The more I thought about it, the more it became apparent that at question was my very competence as a father. After all, what self-respecting father would fail to teach his child such an important life lesson as financial responsibility? The fact that I had been a stockbroker and financial analyst and had handled hundreds of millions of dollars for my clients, and yet had failed to teach my very own daughter the basics of money management caused me to reassess my preparedness for parenthood altogether — albeit about 13 years too late.

After thoroughly berating myself and discounting my worth as a human being, I began to think about the implications of this disturbing yet certainly common parent/child confrontation. Did this mean that my own beloved daughter — the child of a former Wall Street investment advisor, no less — had no concept of the value of money? Had $10 become such an insignificant amount of money that to lose it was like losing a button or a hair barrette? Was losing a $10 bill so insignificant that a 12-year-old could ask for another $10 just as easily as one might ask for another stick of gum five minutes after having been given a stick whose flavor had been "all chewed up?" Exactly how much was $10 worth in the mind of a 12-year-old girl in the waning days of the 20th century?

As the species commonly called parent is instinctively given to do in such situations, I began almost immediately to percolate with semi-clear memories of a time wrapped neatly in the charming fog of nostalgia, a time that is almost always recalled with the prefatory incantation: I remember (with the help of a 20th century almanac laying on the coffee table) when I was your age . . . .

Exactly how much was $10 worth in the mind of a 12-year-old girl in the waning days of the 20th century?

* * *

The year was 1955. Dwight D. Eisenhower was swept into the White House on the strength of a promise to become tougher on communism all over the world and to end the war in Korea. James Dean's *Rebel Without A Cause* opened four days after the teen idol was tragically killed in a car accident; *I*

In 1955 . . .

James Dean's *Rebel Without A Cause* opened, and *I Love Lucy* was the most watched TV program . . .

Love Lucy was the most watched television program; Elvis Presley had his first number one hit; the Brooklyn Dodgers won their first ever World Series; and roller skating and hula hoops were all the rage.

It was in 1955 that Rosa Parks refused to relinquish her seat on a bus to a white man in Montgomery, Alabama; Jonas Salk's polio vaccine was licensed; Disneyland opened in California; The Mickey Mouse Club aired its first episode; former jazz pianist Ray A. Kroc persuaded Richard and Maurice McDonald to let him license their San Bernadino, California roadside fast-food hamburger stand nationally, and opened the first McDonald's franchise in a Chicago suburb.

The same year that IBM introduced its first business computer, both software designer Bill Gates and Apple computer inventor Steven Jobs were born; Nobel Prize-winning physicist Albert Einstein, jazz legend Charlie "Bird" Parker, and pitching great Cy Young all died.

Play-Doh, the Ford Thunderbird, Kentucky Fried Chicken and televised presidential press conferences were introduced that year.

In 1955, the federal debt was $274.4 billion, $226.6 billion of which was held by the public — or about $1,373 per person; the interest paid on the debt constituted 7.1% of total federal outlays. A little over $9 billion ($9.15 billion) was spent on advertising in the U.S. for a population of around 165 million Americans, or $55.45 per person. The Gross National Product (GNP) for 1955 was $398 billion, or about $2,412.12 per person. The minimum wage was raised from 75¢ to $1.

* * *

In 1965 . . .

In 1965, Lyndon Johnson escalated American involvement in Viet Nam. *The Sound of Music* won the Oscar for best picture of 1965; *Bonanza* was the most watched television program; and Frank Sinatra won a Grammy for "It Was a Very Good Year".

1965 brought us the miniskirt, soft contact lenses, Nutra-Sweet, the indoor sports stadium (the Astrodome), and the lava lamp; Harvard professor Timothy Leary coined the phrase "Tune in, turn on, drop out"; in San Francisco, a folk-rock band called The Warlocks, soon to be renamed The Grateful Dead, was formed; and in St. Louis, the Gateway Arch was completed.

That year Cesar Chavez succeeded in organizing American agricultural workers; The Great Society introduced Medicare, food stamps, Head Start, VISTA, and the Job Corps; Ralph Nader began his consumer advocacy crusade; Dr. Martin Luther King led a march from Selma to Montgomery, Alabama; 10,000 angry black Americans, fed up with poverty and unemployment, turned the Los Angeles inner-city neighborhood of Watts into a war zone; and Soviet cosmonaut Aleksei Leonov became the first man to walk in space, followed two months later by American astronaut Edward White.

> Designer Andre Courreges shocked the world when he introduced the miniskirt.

"We are in favor of a detente, but if anybody thinks that for this reason we shall forget about Marx, Engles and Lenin, he is mistaken. This will happen when shrimps learn to whistle."

— Nikita Krushchev

A power outage plunged some 80,000 square miles of New England into darkness and left 30 million people without electricity for over 13 hours; star quarterback Joe Namath snubbed the NFL and signed with the upstart AFL New York Jets for a record $400,000 contract;

Popular singer Nat "King" Cole, British Prime Minister Winston Churchill, comedian Stan Laurel, civil rights leader Malcolm X, pioneering news broadcaster Edward R. Murrow, and missionary Albert Schweitzer all died that year.

That same year, the federal debt was $322.3 billion, $260.8 billion of which was held by the public — or about $1,373 per person; the interest paid on the debt constituted 7.3% of total federal outlays. Advertisers spent $15.25 billion in the U.S. on a population of around 190 million Americans, or about $80.26 per American. The Gross National Product was $684.9 billion, or about $3,604.73 per person.

* * *

In 1975 . . .

In 1975, Gerald Ford took over as president after Richard Nixon resigned under threat of impeachment. *One Flew Over the Cuckoo's Nest* won the Oscar for best picture; *All in the Family* was the most watched television program; Bruce Springsteen, Elton John and The Captain and Tennille were atop the music charts; and disco, platform shoes and Cher were beginning their assault on America.

In 1975, Arthur Ashe became the first black man to win the men's singles championship at Wimbledon. Spain's dictator Francisco Franco died; civil war broke out in Beirut; Saigon fell to the communists; former Teamsters president Jimmy Hoffa disappeared; Lynette "Squeaky" Fromm and Sara

Jane Moore both tried to shoot the President; on the verge of bankruptcy, New York City received a $2 billion federal bailout; home computers were introduced that year, as was light beer, computerized supermarket checkouts, disposable razors, and catalytic converters.

Ethiopian emperor Haile Selassie, Greek shipping magnate Aristotle Onassis, baseball legend Casey Stengel, and *Twilight Zone* creator Rod Serling all died in 1975.

In that same year, the federal debt was $541.9 billion, $394.7 billion of which was carried by the public, or about $1,836 per person; the interest paid on the debt constituted 7% of total federal outlays. The most significant increase in the national debt since World War II, the government took in $279.1 billion and spent $332.3 billion. (In fact, only once in modern history, in 1960, has the government taken in more than they have spent.)

In 1975, $28.16 billion was spent on advertising in the U.S. on a population of about 215 million, or about $130.98 per American. The Gross National Product (GNP) was $1.6 trillion, or about $7,441.86 per person.

Only once in modern history, in 1960, has the government taken in more than they have spent.

* * *

In 1985 . . .

In 1985, Ronald Reagan was in his second term and promising to cut taxes and to balance the national budget. *Out of Africa* won the Oscar for best picture; *The Cosby Show* won an Emmy for best comedy series; the Police, Dire Straits, Whitney Houston, and Tina Turner were atop the pop music charts; Larry McMurtry's *Lonesome Dove* topped the bestseller lists; and Pete Rose broke Ty Cobb's record of 4,191 career hits.

An extra
second was
added to the
calendar
year.

Mikhail Gorbachev became the Soviet leader; British meteorologists confirmed that there was a hole in the ozone layer above Antarctica; South African President P.W. Botha declared martial law when anti-apartheid forces began to fight; and Daniel Ortega was Nicaragua's first popularly elected president in modern times.

Also in 1985, a Greenpeace trawler was sunk by the French government; cocaine production rose by a third and gained acceptance among American young urban professionals (Yuppies); terrorism attacks increased sharply all over the world, including the high jacking of a TWA airliner en route from Rome to Athens; U.S. Naval officer John Walker, Jr. was convicted of spying for the Soviet union; and AIDS claimed the life of film star Rock Hudson.

That year, the Coca-Cola Company introduced "New" Coke which failed miserably; an extra second was added to the calendar year; Nintendo video games, the Rock 'n' Roll Hall of Fame, and a U.S. ban on leaded gas all made their first appearance in 1985.

Actor Yul Brenner, painter Marc Chagall, Soviet Leader Konstantin Chernenko, and actor, director, and film-maker Orson Welles all died.

In that same year, the federal debt was $1.8 trillion, $1.5 trillion of which was held by the public, or about $6,329 per person; the interest paid on the debt constituted 13.7% of total federal outlays. Advertisers spent $94.75 billion on a U.S. population of about 237 million, or about $400 per American. The Gross National Product (GNP) was $4.05 trillion, or about $17,088 per person.

* * *

In 1995, Bill Clinton was president. *Braveheart* won the Oscar for best picture; *Frazier* won an Emmy for best television comedy series; Madonna won an MTV Video Music Award for "Take A Bow"; Hootie & the Blowfish were atop the music charts; the Dallas Cowboys won the Super Bowl; and the Houston Rockets won the NBA Championship.

That year O.J. Simpson was acquitted of murdering his ex-wife Nicole Brown and her friend Ronald Goldman; in April, a truck bomb blew up the federal building in Oklahoma City killing 168 people.

Joseph Rotblat, a Manhattan Project physicist, was awarded The Nobel Peace Prize for his 40 year campaign to eliminate nuclear weapons; the Nobel Prize for Economics went to Robert Lucas, Jr. whose work challenged the Keynesian belief that the government is able to fine-tune the economy; F. Sherwood Roland, Mario Molina, and Paul Crutzen won the Nobel Prize for Chemistry for their pioneering work in explaining how chlorofluorocarbons deplete the ozone layer.

In that same year, the federal debt was $4.921 trillion, $3.603 trillion of which was carried by the public, or about $13,858 per person; the interest paid on the debt constituted 15.3 percent of total federal outlays.

Advertisers spent $160.9 billion in the U.S. on a population of about 260 million people, or about $618 per American.

*   *   *

Yes, when I was your age, I thought silently to my lovely daughter, the world was a much different place to live in — at least as far as scientific and

> In 1995 . . .
>
> The Nobel Prize for Economics went to Robert Lucas, Jr., whose work challenged the Keynesian belief that the government is able to fine-tune the economy.

technological advances are concerned (and of course professional athletes' salaries).

But beyond that, beyond the ever-changing face of the world, is it really such a different place? Are the fundamental principles that have guided us as a society and culture the same now as they were 50 years ago? Underneath the very latest hairstyles and make-ups and fashions, do we still hold the same ideas sacred?

Underneath the very latest hairstyles and make-ups and fashions, do we still hold the same ideas sacred?

In recent years, great strides have been made in correcting some of the mistakes that were made years ago when the conse-quences of many of our actions weren't fore-seen.

It's clear that in the last 50 years, human achievement has reached a level that is unprecedented in the history of civilization. And in recent years, great strides have been made as far as correcting some of the mistakes that we made years ago when the consequences of many of our actions, for whatever reason, weren't foreseen. But perhaps the most striking revelation of the past half century is the fact that, while it's true we have made remarkable progress toward a more enlightened, humane world, it has been expensive — both in abstract humanitarian terms and in concrete financial terms.

Since the beginning of time, progress has had costs — both direct and indirect. When economically advanced nations moved from agrarian-based societies to industrialized societies, one of the monetary prices to be paid was for the machines that characterized that era's progress; one of the abstract costs that society had to bear was the loss of close-knit communities and sense of tangible control over day-to-day life that comes from an increasingly mechanistic social environment. The same type of costs had to be born during the transformation from an industrial society to an informational one. In fact, similar costs had to be born millions of years ago when, in order to survive the draughts and famines and the encroaching savannas, primates left their trees for the open plains and more plentiful food supplies. While it must have been difficult to adjust to new dangers and threats for the adventurous monkeys, it must have been even more difficult for those who decided to stay in their trees when the last banana was eaten.

The psychological price that society pays for progress is frequently unimaginable until after the fact, and may very well be so expensive that the collective psyche of society undergoes a dramatic change to accommodate it. It is with the question of what is lost in order to make room for progress that I am here concerned with, for it's directly related to the confusion I had when my daughter innocently asked me for another $10 to replace the $10 she had lost.

The psycho-logical price that society pays for progress is frequently unimaginable until after the fact.

As an example, consider the moon-landing. Before we landed on the moon, heavenly bodies were the subject of supposition and mystery. Once its surface had been graced by human footsteps, the romance and mystery gave way to science and reason — at least for the vast majority of us. The moon missions signaled the dawn of a new age, of technological advancement, of previously undreamed of scientific possibility — of progress.

The recent Mars Pathfinder mission takes the same idea one step further — and is, no doubt, the natural progression of the space program. Scientists are speculating about the existence of life on the red planet. Chances are that the Pathfinder mission will not confirm this, and perhaps then progress will point toward more down to earth issues — and may even squelch the "new mythologies" that the space program gave birth to, such as can be seen regularly on the *X Files* — thus bringing full-circle the cycle of progress, including the spin-off mythologies that it inevitably generates.

For another example, we have only to look so far as electronic self-service ATM gas pumps. Once upon a time, you could pull in to a gas station, the attendant would rush out and, while filling the tank up, check your oil, clean your windshield, maybe even have some candy for the kids in the back seat. Now, however, the only human you're likely to see is the clerk behind the counter who simply wants to know which pump you used. Gone are the days of your friendly man with a star — a genuine real live human who is more familiar with your automobile than you are. On a more abstract level, the loss of service station attendants embodied the inevitable trend toward the hyper-active-always-in-a-hurry culture we're in the throes of now (along with TV and microwave dinners and time saving appliances, etc.). Of course, it may be successfully argued that Americans have always been given to impatience and having things "now" and having them just the way they want them (it is, after all, how our country began in the first place).

Another example — and no doubt one that is probably closer to the issue that I'm here concerned with — is the wide-spread use of credit cards and ATM cards and other devices that make paying for things so easy. By being able to get things so easily, seemingly without having to pay cash for them, the message that many of us take from this — especially children since they're not the ones paying the bills at the end of the month — is that money isn't so

It may be successfully argued that Americans have always been given to impatience and having things now and having them just the way they want them (it is, after all, how our country began in the first place).

important. In fact, it's not even necessary when it comes right down to it. You just pull out a piece of plastic and whatever you want is yours. Our sense of value, of delayed gratification, of worth — all have been manipulated by the convenience that plastic offers. Coupled with the massive and almost unbearably seductive marketing mentality that naturally accompanies consumerism.

It's possible that the massive socio-economic blossoming we've come through in the last 50 years has obscured the fundamental financial principles that, no doubt, were instrumental to progress in the first place. Or has progress introduced something much more insidious: has it so eclipsed the achievements of the past that our collective memory of it has been erased.

Or has progress introduced something much more insidious: has it so eclipsed the achievements of the past that our collective memory of it has been erased.

Certainly it couldn't be that I've simply neglected my own children's financial education, assuming that those skills would just come naturally, because I've been too caught up in progress myself. Whatever the culprit, there are some interesting observations to be made about progress and its march through the last half of the 20th century.

* * *

The amount advertisers have spent to get us to buy things has increased over 1,700% since 1955.

By 1987, America had more shopping malls than high schools.

Since 1955, our national debt has increased almost 1,600%; our gross domestic product has increased by over 1,000%; and the amount advertisers have spent to get us to buy things has increased over 1,700%! The thing that is more staggering to me than anything else about these figures is that the only thing increasing more than our debt is the amount of money we spend to make us want more things. While productivity has definitely increased at an amazing clip, debt and expenditures to separate us from our money have increased at an even more amazing clip.

Some other interesting observations about the world we have created: by 1987, America had more shopping malls than high schools; by the age of 20, the average person will have seen a million commercial messages; 40% of all mail is advertising, and by the end of the average person's life span, he or she will have spent one whole year watching commercials. Right here in Colorado (Colorado Springs, to be precise), there are soft drink company, fast food chain, and sneaker manufacturer ads in school hallways and on the sides of school buses.

And how has all this effected our spending patterns and buying habits? There are over a billion credit cards in the U.S.; credit card debt tripled in the 80s. Also in that decade, there were an unprecedented number of bankruptcies declared. Americans save on average a piddly 5% of their income; compare that to the Japanese who save over 10%. There is a game on the market designed to whet children's appetites for shopping: the winner is the one who buys the most stuff and gets to the parking lot without spilling their purchases.

And how does this rampant consumerism effect our world? Since 1950, Americans have used more natural resources than all the people who have lived before them combined; each of us use on average 20 tons of natural resources in a lifetime. We throw away 7 million cars annually — the crowning achievement of a marketing concept popularized in the 1950s, "planned obsolescence." If every country in the world were as affluent as the United States, we would be smack in the middle of a global disaster. Yet this is the goal of an optimum global economy.

* * *

It doesn't take a Nobel prize-winning economist to see that the 21st century is approaching with enough economic strength to buy and sell nations. As a species, we've conceived of, built, bought and sold more in the 20th century than in the 19 previous centuries combined. By Year 2000, we will have spent more in this decade than in the previous nine decades put together.

By Year 2000, we will have spent more in this decade than in the previous nine decades put together.

Yet the majority of Americans — 80% according to the experts — don't understand basic financial concepts such as the prime interest rate, compound interest, or IRA accounts. If it's true — and I believe it is — that our personal financial sophistication is an accurate reflection of our national financial predicament, then it's little wonder that we have a mon-

Since 1950, Americans have used more natural resources than all the people who have lived before them combined.

As a species, we've conceived of, built, bought and sold more in the 20th century than in the 19 previous centuries combined.

If the U.S.A. were a private individual, it would have long ago been arrested for bouncing checks — or at the very least, would have been forced to declare bankruptcy.

strous national debt. If the U.S.A. were a private individual, it would have long ago been arrested for bouncing checks — or at the very least, would have been forced to declare bankruptcy.

If past history is any indication of our collective ability to change the course we're on, one thing is clear: all the political posturing and promising in the world is not going to change economic behavioral patterns. Like most behaviors, financial management has traditionally been learned by watching those who have gone before. In the case of our children, those being watched are most often parents.

True, political action can change the rules and adjust the playing board, but what is at question here is behavior, plain and simple. And until we learn how to change our behavior as it regards financial responsibility, there's little hope of changing the collision course with financial ruin we're on — both collectively as a society and, for a great many of us, individually. And behavior is something that can only be changed by education, application and experience. Consequently, if we're to change the way we manage our financial situation in an effective and responsible way, it must be at a very early age and in a solidly pragmatic manner. It seems apparent that for the next generation to have any chance at all to succeed in an economic environment of aggressive growth and hyper-activity, more thoughtful and responsible money management skills must be taught to our children now.

* * *

Clearly our socio-economic environment has changed a great deal since I was born. While many may rightly argue that the values and ideals needed to succeed in any social environment are a constant, the forces that interact with and against those values and ideals have become powerfully refined and increasingly intrusive. Our consumer attitudes are constantly assaulted by psychologically powerful, need-creating consumerism. The thin line between the things we want and the things we need is perpetually challenged by a culture in the throes of virtual technology and its accompanying media marketing blitz. The feeling of being left behind is frequently overwhelming to the point of immobilization.

It's mind-numbing to imagine what the world my children are growing up in will look like 15, 10, even five years from now. I fully expect one of my children to visit me 25 years from now and comment on Dad's antique gasoline-powered car, or Mom's old-fashioned cellular phone without video, or those simply dreadful-sounding old CDs they used to put music on when she was a little girl. When one considers the hyper-aggressive nature of progress over the last 25 years, and the fact that important new cutting edge technology is being developed every day for public use tomorrow, it's not unreasonable to assume that the future will be just as astonishing to our children then as the present is to us now.

There's no question that the demands of the future upon those fortunate enough to see it will be great. New challenges and opportunities not yet imagined are sure to face us. To succeed in such a promising yet uncertain world will take no small amount of preparation. The obvious question, then, is how does one prepare for a world that is sure to be different from anything we can imagine? The answer is that it takes strong, fundamentally sound principles and a thoughtful philosophy of life management that, like any philosophy should, works under any circumstances.

> The thin line between the things we want and the things we need is perpetually challenged by a culture in the throes of virtual technology and its accompanying media marketing blitz.

In a recent national address, President Clinton echoed the sentiments of an increasing number of Americans by chastising congress for dragging its feet and skirting the issues on legislation that would, "Give people the tools they need to make their own lives." He went on to reaffirm his commitment to the pursuit of opportunity, and warned against inaction by saying that, "The enemy of our times is inaction."

"The enemy of our times is inaction."

— President Clinton

Regardless of one's political affiliation, the ideas he expressed are right on target. I can't stress in strong enough terms the importance of teaching kids about money. Not only is it a skill that will hopefully go a long way toward helping them live a happy and more fulfilled life, but raising future generations of more financially responsible citizens is an absolute necessity if we as a culture are to survive and flourish in the next millennium.

Resources

Books

All the Money in the World, by Bill Brittain (HarperCollins Children's Books). Boy gets wish of having all the money in the world, with disasterous consequences. (intermediate)

Films

Consumer Reports: Buy Me That; *Buy Me That Too*; *Buy Me That 3*. The series looks into advertising aimed at children. *Buy Me That* and *Buy Me That 3* available from Films Incorporated, (800) 343-4312; *Buy Me That Too* available from Ambrose Video (800) 526-4663.

Software

A-Train (MAXIS). Fledgling empire builders create a railroad, then a city, and strive to show a profit.

DinoPark Tycoon (MECC). Children operate their own business as they build a dinosaur theme park. (primary to adult)

The Oregon Trail (MECC). Adventurers travel by covered wagon from Independence, MO to Oregon. Along the way they learn how to shop for and buy the supplies they need and make their money last the trip.

Games

Roup (Porter Planet-3 Games; P.O. Box 773, Smethport, PA   16749; $28.50 plus $3 shipping). Players bid in rubles for 39 properties, such as the Kremlin, Red Square, the Lenin Mausoleum and KGB headquarters. The game ends when all money has been transferred from the Old Communist Bank to the New Democracy Bank and all properties have been sold to private owners. (late primary and up)

Watchdog Organizations

The Children's Advertising Unit (CARU). Established by the advertising industry to promote responsible children's advertising and to respond to public concerns, the organization publishes *A Parent's Guide: Advertising and Your Child*, which discusses how you can monitor and explain advertising to your children; and for advertisers, *Self-Regulatory Guidelines for Children's Advertising*. To order, contact: CARU, 845 Third Avenue, NY, NY 10022; (212) 754-1354.

Organizations and Associations

Junior Achievement works with schools and businesses to introduce students to practical economic concepts, business organization, management, production and marketing. For more information, write or call: Junior Achievement, 45 East Clubhouse Dr., Colorado Springs, CO 80906; (719) 540-8000.

Chapter 2

Life Management

A little over 200 years ago our founding fathers set forth the ideals and elements necessary for the management of a grand new government by the people and for the people. While it's still early and the grand new government is young by comparison to some of the venerable European countries, all indications are that it has and will continue to be a monumental success — as of yet unmatched in the history of civilizations. No doubt due in large part to the visionary ideals and elements of that document of social management, our country has flourished beyond anyone's wildest dreams. The principles of freedom and equality — even though at times in our history those principles have been severely tested by our own developing nature — have given birth to a fertile spirit that has taken progress — in all its myriad forms — to unprecedented levels. Our civilization has become the most productive in human history, and we as a culture are both reaping the benefits and suffering the consequences of our own nature.

Our civilization has become the most productive in human history, and we as a culture are both reaping the benefits and suffering the consequences of our own nature.

As we enter the new millennium and struggle to come to terms with what we have wrought, it's clear that future survival will require basic life management skills to not only cope with the world outside, but how we manage ourselves. Clearly it will be a long and complicated journey, and those of us who survive and flourish along the way will no doubt be as prepared as possible for whatever may come. It only follows that a sound life management philosophy is what future survival calls for — one that, much like our own social management philosophy, incorporates all the ideals and elements that will not only allow, but facilitate growth and success.

It's clear that future survival will require basic life management skills to not only cope with the world outside, but how we manage ourselves.

Since the beginning of civilization, there have been innumerable "life management" philosophies and the like — some of them brilliant, some crack pot. The point is that mankind has always recognized the need to have some sort of guide or map to live by. As we as a species have evolved socially, some of these life management philosophies have evolved with the changing times; many more have not. We need not look very far to see the effects of the inability to change with the times. Consider the recent break-up of the Soviet bloc countries and the move toward a free market economy and democratic government in the former USSR; or in more ancient times, Greece, Rome and virtually every other civilization whose inability to cope with progress and thus the future interests of its people, has resulted in the eventual fall of powerful empires and governments.

Even our own society — as well suited for adjusting to what the public wants — has not been exempt from the failure to adjust to the changing times: the Civil War was a response to the changing times — or rather the lack thereof; the Great Depression was a result of the inability of both an economic system and a government to address the issues of the changing face of society; the civil rights movement and the women's liberation movement and the anti-war movement — for that matter, the 60s in general — were a response to the changing face of our society. The force that is most responsible for the changing times we live in now is the technological revolution.

The force that is most responsible for the changing times we live in now is the technological revolution.

If we're to continue to grow and evolve along the same lines as society, and participate in our own remarkable social process, it's essential that we incorporate a personal life management philosophy into our lives that will work for us no matter what circumstances we may encounter in the future. Such a life management model, by definition, should help one manage the various aspects of a life using basic principles that will serve as a foundation for decision-making and policy-setting.

Physical Health and Well-Being

The first element of a life management model is physical well-being. Without this fundamental element, all else is pointless. Unfortunately, many of us don't enjoy this most basic of human needs. Even in an industrialized country like China, only 69% of the population has access to safe water, and only a minute 16% has access to sanitation. In Cambodia, 53% of the population has access to health services, 36% have access to safe water, and 14% of the population has access to sanitation. Even in our North American neighbor, Mexico, only 78% of the population has access to health services. In countries like Afghanistan and Somalia and Rwanda, life expectancy is in the mid-forties and in some cases, it has actually decreased in the last 25 years.

Even the richest, most socially developed country in the world is not immune to serious health problems: in 1996, 501,310 cases of AIDS were reported in the United States (the next highest, Brazil, reported 71,111 cases). Granted, as a percentage of the population, there are many countries with a higher rate — some countries in Africa report that nearly 20% of their population are infected with AIDS. Another health problem that usually receives a scoff or a smile when mentioned, is calorie intake. Only

Even in an industrialized country like China, only 69% of the population has access to safe water, and only a minute 16% has access to sanitation.

In 1996, 501,310 cases of AIDS were reported in the United States (the next highest, Brazil, reported 71,111 cases).

The United States has a coronary heart disease rate that is seven times higher than Japan's (which is the lowest among industrialized countries).

Greece and North Korea have higher average daily calorie intake than the United States. In industrialized nations, cardiovascular diseases cause over half of all deaths. The United States has a coronary heart disease rate that is seven times higher than Japan's (which is the lowest among industrialized countries).

The point of these figures is to illustrate that physical health and well-being — the most basic of human needs and something that we Americans tend to take for granted — is often not the given that we think it is. For many, the struggle to simply stay alive is so overwhelming and all-consuming that other basic needs are neglected — perhaps even ignored. It's only common sense that for a healthy, well-rounded life, one needs a healthy environment wherein personal health and physical growth are stressed. Without this basic necessity, chances are that emotional well-being, intellectual growth, social interaction and other essential aspects of personality development may not develop properly. For this reason, physical health and well-being are the foundation upon which the life management philosophy I propose is built.

Emotional Health and Well-Being

The second element is emotional health and well-being. Without a safe, supportive environment, it's unlikely that the proper emotional development necessary for further personality development will occur. Granted, collectively we've made great strides in the past 50 years in realizing the importance of a healthy emotional environment. Still, hardly a day passes when there's not a story on the evening news or in the newspaper about emotional neglect and abuse. What's even more disturbing are the stories that aren't reported — the ones that happen in virtually every neighborhood and every school. All too often children are raised in a home environment that resembles a war zone. Fifty percent of marriages end in divorce; over 30% of children under 18 live with one (or less) parent; over 3 million Americans are homeless, roughly the population of Colorado.

Of course these are only a few of the manifestations of an unhealthy emotional environment. The more subtle manifestations may be all but invisible to the untrained eye, but every bit as stifling as more dramatic emotional problems. Many of them are problems associated with "progress" and the social patterns and values passed down from apparently healthy family environments (at least what has always been considered healthy and even admirable values). So preoccupied with success and material and creature comforts are many of us, that the time we have for our children — quality time — seems harder and harder to find. The result is that we fail to provide a supportive, creative family environment, and the lack thereof can alienate our children from not only us, but society as a whole. When people feel alienated, they tend to create an environment that, at least for the time being, fulfills their immediate needs. Usually when this happens they turn inward and neglect personal relationships which stifles social skills and inhibits further emotional development.

For better or worse, progress has created many problems in the area of emotional well-being. It's not uncommon for children — and adults, for that matter — who have not been nurtured in a healthy, creative environment to turn away from overwhelming new experiences which can further exacerbate an already tentative emotional environment. Not only

Fifty percent of marriages end in divorce; over 30% of children under 18 live with one (or less) parent; over 3 million Americans are homeless, roughly the population of Colorado.

A healthy emotional environment builds confidence and fosters a more vital learning situation.

do children need to be introduced caringly to new experiences, but they need an attentive, supportive environment in which to process new experiences. Experiencing new things with children can also be a healthy emotional situation for the parents. In our hyper-accelerated society, it's essential that parents spend quality time with their children, and vice-versa. A healthy emotional environment builds confidence and fosters a more vital learning situation. Which brings me to the next element: a healthy intellectual environment.

Intellectually Supportive Environment

Given a safe and physically healthy existence and an emotionally supportive environment, it's incumbent upon parents to provide an atmosphere conducive to intellectual stimulation — and by this I don't mean just encouraging them to do well in school. What I'm talking about here is providing the necessary environment whereby children learn how to learn.

> What I'm talking about here is providing the necessary environment whereby children learn how to learn.

In a culture where last year's version of a software program is all but obsolete, it's important that children develop a pragmatic foundation of learning skills and a functional system of processing information so that they can not only keep up with the ever-expanding world we live in, but take advantage of its opportunities and possibilities.

Most likely we all have friends and family members who grew up in a time when preparing for the future meant simply learning a skill or trade that was useful, or maybe getting a college degree. Those days are gone forever. How many of us are just now realizing that computer skills are almost a requirement for existence? And how many of us still don't know how to use the Internet? There is no doubt that there will be something in the store next week that we couldn't even imagine last week. There's virtually no area that technology has not touched in the last ten years. What's more, a whole new technology vernacular has found its way into everyday language. Our children come home from school using words that didn't exist six months ago.

Of course, this phenomenon is nothing new; since the beginning of time, our threshold for comprehending has been recreated time and time again. Imagine the leap that was required by the invention of the electric light bulb, or the "One small step for man, and one giant leap for mankind." The idea of a man walking on the moon was, 50 or 60 years ago, perhaps as unbelievable as private spaceships are to us today. It's all too obvious that the only way we as a society can survive is if we prepare ourselves for the inevitable: progress. For it may be that we're just now capable of understanding that this is how things work — that progress is the natural state of a healthy world. No longer are we as a species easily amazed by human achievement; we must incorporate this idea — the capacity to accept the fact that the world as we know it will, no doubt, change many times within our lifetime — into our intellectual infrastructure.

> Imagine the leap that was required by the invention of the electric light bulb, or the "One small step for man, and one giant leap for mankind."

One of the great dangers we face intellectually in our culture is the trend toward time- and energy-saving technology. Granted, many of the developments over the last 50 years have made tedious and unpleasant tasks much more manageable and have freed up a considerable amount of our time — time that can be spent on more fulfilling pursuits. But for many of us, these time- and energy-saving developments have had the effect of making many tasks and projects so quick and easy to accomplish by simply flipping a switch or punching a button that fundamental skills are neglected and we never internalize a basic understanding of many essential functions. We've seen this with calculators and mathematics, televisions and reading, and computer programs and problem solving. For the most part, progress has made life better for the vast majority of us; unfortunately a dangerous side effect of progress is that it has also created an environment wherein thinking for ourselves is becoming an endangered skill.

It's important that we not only insist upon a solid grasp of rudimentary knowledge and skills — fundamental knowledge and skills that can and should be applied to virtually every situation, no matter how simple or complicated — but it's equally important that we provide a stimulating environment that nurtures and challenges intellectual exploration. An environment that exposes children to new experiences will open doors to new interests and opportunities. That, coupled with a solid foundation that allows for the assimilation of new experiences, ideas and knowledge will create a stimulating environment for intellectual growth — essential if our children are to participate in the challenging world that awaits them.

An environment that exposes children to new experiences will open doors to new interests and opportunities.

Personal Health and Well-Being

One of the things that has plagued many of us who have, for the most part, adapted well to our fast-paced socio-cultural environment is personal health problems. Of all the industrialized countries in the world, the United States has by far the highest coronary heart disease rate — seven times higher than Japan's. There are many factors that contribute to this astounding figure — including dietary habits, job/career-related stress and anxiety, relational stress and anxiety, and the stress and anxiety that comes from social expectations, both real and imagined. It would not be incorrect to say that progress has played a major role in the personal physical and mental health of our society. Notorious for our do-everything-on-the-go mentality, often we get so caught up in being successful and accomplishing great things that we neglect even more important things like our own health. It doesn't take a sociologist to see that progress can have an expensive price tag — both physiologically and psychologically. It's not a new phenomenon by any stretch of the imagination; it is, however, perhaps more culturally threatening now than at any time in history. The demands placed on our psyche by an accelerated cultural environment and the subsequent physiological toll those demands take is frequently overwhelming to the point of causing serious mental and physical problems.

In recent years there has been a trend, not only in the United States, but all over the world, toward physical fitness and acknowledging its importance not only for mental performance but also for emotional health. In fact, one of the great achievements in health and medicine in the last 25 years is that

> It doesn't take a sociologist to see that progress can have an expensive price tag — both physiologically and psychologically.

The pace of progress over the last 25 years has eclipsed that of even the industrial revolution.

people are starting to take more responsibility for their own health. So much so that the popularity of health and fitness has given birth to a vital and flourishing industry. There has also been an unprecedented blossoming of popular spirituality, ranging from thoughtful holistic meditations and lifestyles to intense focus on crystals and mathematical studies of heavenly bodies, from self-proclaimed prophetic gurus to mystically gifted animals. If it's true that social and cultural evolution, by its own nature, occurs at precisely the rate it's supposed to and according to its own laws and logic, it's no wonder these trends are upon us now. The pace of progress over the last 25 years has eclipsed that of even the industrial revolution; the developments in science, technology and communications have created and recreated the face of our society many times over. The accompanying frenetic cyclical processes of adjusting to the ever-changing face of our society frequently leaves many of us overwhelmed, burnt out, and disoriented. For obvious reasons, it's essential that we instill a strong commitment to a healthy body and mind in a philosophy that seeks to manage how we survive and flourish in such a cultural atmosphere. Such a commitment will help pull together and solidify the disparate elements necessary for a well-rounded life philosophy that, by design, can help us to realize our potential and lead a more fulfilled life.

Many of the things that we can do to improve our health and well-being are obvious and there's no shortage of publications and programs and word-of-mouth to inform us. Simple common sense will go a long way toward improved health. Whether its running, bicycling, roller blading, golf, tennis, basketball, weightlifting or any number of physical activities, every one of us needs to have some form of physical exercise to keep us vital and alert, both physically and spiritually — and by spiritually I mean that part of our self that responds mentally/intellectually and emotionally to both internal and external stimuli. Which brings me to one of the things that many of us overlook — myself included — in our day-to-day lives as far as health is concerned: emotional well-being.

Unfortunately much of the public attention to health is focused on the physical: What muscles are effected by a certain exercise, etc. Emotional health, which is every bit as important as physical health, has been neglected in the health craze. Without specific attention to emotional well-being, it's unlikely that we will achieve a true state of good health and well-being. In fact, neglecting emotional health may very well be detrimental to physical health. Such a limited view of personal health can only mean limited benefits and, no doubt, limited success with one's life management philosophy.

Social Responsibility

Of course the well-rounded life management philosophy will include the skills and knowledge necessary to participate responsibly in a social environment. Without the ability to participate in the responsible evolution of a particular social environment, the advantages and opportunities available now may not be available to future generations. In fact, many of the problems we face as a society today stem from a lack of the knowledge and skills necessary to address collective, social issues. It's essential that, if we as a society are to survive, that we instill a strong sense of social awareness — one that spawns understanding, facilitates participation, and instills a sense of duty

Many of the problems we face as a society today stem from a lack of the knowledge and skills necessary to address collective, social issues.

and responsibility to improve where improvement is needed.

Frequently in our culture, one of the side effects of the pursuit of "success" is a sort of tunnel vision that allows for little else than what is in the line of vision: that which facilitates success or that which hinders success. Often we become so immersed in our vision of success that we can't see the bigger picture or even our part in it.

Recently, there was a politician running for national office. A self-made millionaire in business and well respected attorney, he had handled some of the most high profile, difficult cases dealing with environmental issues and business interests. After successfully defending several large corporations against environmental law suits, and saving those corporations millions of dollars, he decided to throw his name in the hat. Running on a platform that included labeling himself as an environmentalist, and generally viewed as the odds-on favorite to win, he was narrowly defeated, largely because of his record of defending what were seen by the voting public as corporate environmental marauders. The obvious message here is that the public expects its leaders to practice what they preach.

In recent years it has become good business to promote social responsibility as an integral part of the corporate philosophy.

In recent years it has become good business to promote social responsibility as an integral part of the corporate philosophy.

Granted, this often is done purely as a marketing strategy and has little if any truth to it in so far as the way a certain company may conduct its business. Nevertheless, there is a growing number of businesses that have adopted a more socially responsible view of their role in society and have even structured their corporate policies to reflect their organization's commitment. The effect this will have could be dramatic: with companies placing an increased emphasis on social responsibility, it only follows that they will be looking for those same qualities in their employees. Consequently, these qualities will need to be instilled in the future work force — which means your children and mine. Needless to say, this sort of cultural coming of age is long overdue.

Financial Responsibility

Finally, certainly no well-rounded, forward-thinking life management philosophy would overlook personal financial responsibility, and it's with this matter that this book is concerned. For it's apparent from the mistakes of our past, mistakes that have no doubt contributed a great deal to our current national financial irresponsibility, that we as a country, while we may have mastered the art of money-making, have yet to master the art of money management. That more than anything is the impetus behind our nearly $4 trillion national public debt. Individually, had we understood and implemented a sound philosophy of personal money management years ago, it seems likely that those principles would have found their way into the philosophy of at least some of those folks who are responsible for spending taxpayers' money (perhaps the notion that you can't spend more than you make)! Unfortunately, like most of us, they

As a country, we may have mastered the art of money-making, but we have yet to master the art of money management.

The truth is that a sound philosophy of personal financial responsibility should be one of the most important elements of anyone's life management philosophy.

learned their money management skills by watching those who went before them. The result is a tragic repetition of old bad habits and mistakes — if for no other reason than that's the way it's always been done.

The truth is that a sound philosophy of personal financial responsibility should be one of the most important elements of anyone's life management philosophy. Besides the obvious benefit of promoting financial stability and security, a value system that includes sound money management promotes a wide range of other important psycho-social behaviors — both concrete and abstract.

Benefits of Sound Money Management

Education. As with anything intended as a system of organization, there is a good deal of education involved — both in the teaching of the system itself, and from the actual use of it once implemented. Not only is a system by which things may be collected, organized, contemplated and acted upon being installed into one's broader life management philosophy, but a window is being built through which the world around you might be perceived in a more useful light. When you install a new software program on your computer, you not only learn how to perform the actual functions that program enables, but also about the things encountered through the use of those functions. Certainly in any sound money management system, one would learn basic concepts of spending, saving, giving and investing, as well as the necessary tools — checking accounts, savings accounts, IRA accounts, stocks, bonds, etc., — and their purpose within the framework of the system.

Additionally, through proper use of the system, one learns through experience about the social and economic forces that effect the use of these tools, how through experience one is likely to react to those forces and, consequently, about the world in which one's system of organization is applied.

Discipline. One of the most obvious benefits of a sound money management philosophy is discipline. So much of our current personal financial woes can be directly attributed to the lack of discipline. There is perhaps no better teacher of discipline than successfully managing your own financial resources. The degree of learning is substantial since it's predominantly experiential and therefore imprints itself upon one's personality. The simple act of waiting to purchase something until one's budget allows for its purchase — delayed gratification — is strong reinforcement for developing important financial management skills like prioritization, motivation and long-term/big picture point of view — all essential to a sound system of personal financial responsibility and philosophy of life management.

> There is perhaps no better teacher of discipline than successfully managing your own financial resources.

Mental Health. While it's an abstraction that can't be listed on the side of the box as included along with instructions and warranty, mental health may perhaps be the "free prize inside" — albeit invisible — and the most compelling reason of all (aside from the simple ability to sustain some level of financial security) to develop a sound philosophy of financial responsibility. With the percentage of divorces related to financial problems as high as 90%, the anxiety over the astronomical national debt, the increasingly high cost of living and the skyrocketing cost of education, it's essential that individuals take control of their own financial destiny instead of being blown willy-nilly by whatever wind happens to howl.

Psychologists agree that one of the keys to good mental health is being able to take control of the social environment in which you exist instead of letting the environment control you.

Psychologists agree that one of the keys to good mental health is being able to take control of the social environment in which you exist instead of letting the environment control you.

We've all seen people — perhaps even loved ones — who have been unable to take control of the direction their life takes and instead find themselves caught up in and pulled along by whatever predicament they find themselves in. By establishing and following a good money management system, one can take a big step in the direction of taking control of one's life, avoiding the stress and anxiety brought on by financial worries.

In addition to promoting good mental health in your children, their mastery of sound money management skills also reduces a lot of the stress, worry and anxiety that you the parent might have. If a parent can teach child money management skills early on so that they take care of their own finances, the constant requests for money to buy this or that, the advances in allowances and other unwanted monetary requests, are eliminated since the child will have learned that they are responsible for their own financial situation. Mom and Dad are not held emotional hostage to their children's financial irresponsibility.

Why now?

It's clear that most Americans haven't taken the time to instill a strong sense of personal financial responsibility in their children. It's also clear that had a more solid background in financial management been taught to the average American, it's certain that a more healthy economic environment that moves toward full employment, maximum production and economic independence would be the legacy we would pass on to our children. Such a legacy certainly would go a long way toward relieving a lot of the anxiety I have about my own children's prospects for a happy and fulfilled life amidst the staggering national debt that they will have to tackle.

The real question in all this is whether it's too late or not. We've all heard the saying, "You can't teach an old dog new tricks." This is perhaps more true now than ever. Our children have grown accustomed to a world where you point and click and anything imaginable is right in front of them. There are so many frivolous distractions to quality learning, so many alternative scheme-like methods with glitzy graphics and sound-bite mantras that promise to edify, enlighten, and turn Gilligan into Thurston Howell III in six short weeks. The American dream is so commercialized and steeped in our own cultural mysticism that it resembles a TV game show — complete with prizes from sponsors in exchange for promotional considerations and lightening rounds where you can double your money. Frequently parents are just as spellbound and unable to sort through the graphics and endorsements and may not even have the ability to understand the bottom line. Further problems arise when we look to our social and cultural institutions for guidance and leadership.

The American dream is so commercialized and steeped in our own cultural mysticism that it resembles a TV game show — complete with prizes from sponsors in exchange for promotional considerations and lightening rounds where you can double your money.

"If the government can spend more than its allowance, why can't I?" Johnny might insightfully ask.

"If the government can spend more than its allowance, why can't I?" Johnny might insightfully ask.

As a society, we participate in a wide range of practices that would be foolish for our children to emulate. And while both political parties toss politically expedient blame for our astronomical national debt back and forth like a beach volleyball match, the real blame lies safely hidden in the values we were taught at a very young age — values that, by now, are deeply embedded in not only our collective psyche, but in our economic policy, as well.

As we've witnessed in recent years, getting our political leaders to agree on what to do about our national economic situation is difficult at best, let alone for them to actually do something about it. In a representative democracy, political leaders are, in theory at least, representative of the demographic constituency they represent. Sadly, in our country, only a fraction of the eligible voters participate in the political process, so it can hardly be an empirically definitive indication of our national concern over our economic situation.

The question we as Americans are faced with as the new millennium approaches and our national debt nears $4 trillion is: Is it too late to change the path we're on? Of course not. And the time to start teaching personal financial responsibility is when personal skills are being learned, as early as three years old, when kids frequently start asking questions about money and what things cost. The teaching at this age is largely fundamental and much like teaching a puppy not to turn over its water bowl. Nevertheless, the important foundations for more advanced concepts must be laid down first and well. A recent article in *Working Mother* advises that the sooner you begin, the better. Young children are eager to please and learn; therefore it's a good idea to introduce good money habits early on, while they're still easy to reach.

At the same time we're introducing Mary to reading and writing and personal communication skills, we should also be teaching her basic financial management principles.

So. How does Mary get started?

In no uncertain terms, that's how. It's extremely important that children understand that what they're about to do is completely new. Old habits have a way of creeping into new situations. It's absolutely necessary to let it be known that the old way of doing things (if indeed there was an old way of doing things to begin with, as opposed to no way at all) is no longer acceptable, and that everything about the old way should be thrown out, trashed, deleted, forgotten! Otherwise, when certain aspects of the new money management method get a little tricky, or something is temporarily unclear, or the results take longer to see than the child would like, the temptation to fall back into old habits is sometimes too overwhelming and, consequently, the new system is compromised.

New behavior, firmly established in the child's mind as the way things are going to be done from this point on in no uncertain terms, helps Mary begin learning how to be financially responsible. The process by which this will happen is called the Four-Part Money Management System.

> It's extremely important that children understand that what they're about to do is completely new.

The Four-Part
Money Management System

As both a parent and former professional financial advisor, I've watched at times with amusement and at other times with great distress the utterly disorganized and frequently thoughtless way in which money and financial matters have been managed. Over the years I've seen adults make mistakes that, I thought, a child would never make. Unfortunately, when I've tested this by watching my own children and friends' children, I discovered that, indeed, the very same mistakes are made — which tells me that these mistakes are made because most adults weren't taught basic money management skills when they were children. It's at that point that much of the financial chaos that we exist in began to make sense. People just don't know any better.

Certainly to one who has been trained in finance, money management seems simple and straightforward enough. But for most people, it doesn't seem that important, consequently, it's left up to financial advisors and the like. The bottom line is that if something is important enough to hire experts to take care of, it's important enough to, at the very least, learn the basics — if for no other reason than to be able to communicate effectively with the experts you're spending hard-earned money on. It's not so much about the skills, but rather instilling the importance of having those skills.

It's not so much about the skills, but rather instilling the importance of having those skills.

For precisely this reason — that the importance of personal financial responsibility is the key — I've developed what I call the *Four-Part Money Management System*. Essentially, it's a flexible system designed to encompass and expand with the progressive conceptual maturity of your children. Increasingly sophisticated elements of the System are employed as their ability to understand financial concepts grows. It's a behavior-based teaching system that relies on self-rewarding actions that reinforce positive behavior patterns with respect to managing money.

The System is structured around a fixed, regular allowance. Without income, your children have no money with which to practice the management techniques. The four elements of the System — spending, giving, saving, investing — constitute the totality of what can be done with money except hide it or throw it away. The spending and giving elements help to develop the responsible handling of cash outflow. Saving demonstrates the advantages of goal setting and the rewards that accrue when working toward short- and medium-term goals. Investing addresses the benefits of long-term goals and assures your children of a financially secure future. Your children derive an increase in self-confidence and self-esteem from successfully handling their own money while internalizing skills that will last a lifetime.

The four elements of the System — spending, giving, saving, investing — constitute the totality of what can be done with money except hide it or throw it away.

In following chapters, I will discuss each of these in more detail. But before I get into the specifics of the Four-Part Money Management System, a background of money — its history, evolution and importance — is in order.

Resources

Books

Coping With Money, by Richard S. and Mary Price Lee (The Rosen Publishing Group). Offers advice on coping with money issues. (teens)

Chapter 3

What is Money?

What is
money if not
a tool to
accomplish
something
else.

In what scientists now believe to be the two and half million year history of mankind (a recent archaeological excavation in Ethiopia produced the oldest human-made tools ever discovered), the role of money has been as fundamentally important as tools themselves. In fact, what is money if not a tool to accomplish something else. It has no real value or importance in and of itself; its only value is as a means to an end — a representative of value in a system that recognizes it as having value. Whether it be used to enlist labor or purchase materials or other tools to build a house or build a bridge, to buy a ticket to a movie or play that will, hopefully, amuse, entertain, enlighten, or otherwise benefit, or to buy a lunch or dinner to nourish, relieve hunger pangs, or get to know someone special a little better, the money one uses is only a tool to accomplish a thing that, to the one who uses it, is more valuable than the money it takes to accomplish it. In what has been no small intellectual revolution, humankind has, for whatever reason, been able to make the jump from a concrete perception of tools to an abstract one. For as much that reason as any other one in our psycho-social development, we have survived and flourished as a species beyond even our own wildest dreams. Money has perhaps been the single most important tool that humankind has used.

> Money has perhaps been
> the single most important tool that
> humankind has used.

The concept of money is inextricably linked to the idea of bartering, the impact of which was immediate and far reaching. As nomadic tribes in search of food happened upon one another, they exchanged skins and animals and even tools which, they hoped, would improve their life in some way, whether it be an advancement in technology as far as the tools were concerned, or a better tasting small animal than their staple, roasted iguana (or some such). Eventually improvements in agriculture spawned more geographically stable societies. As permanent dwelling villages and towns and cities sprang up, the need for a place where goods and services could be exchanged arose, and thus began the first public marketplaces where buyers and sellers could come together conveniently. Merchants would travel far and wide to acquire goods that could be bartered in the open market.

Items that were used for early money included tea leaves, shells, feathers, animal teeth, tobacco, blankets and liquor.

This system worked well for a long time. Problems arose, however, when one trader had nothing the other wanted or could not agree what a fair trade for his mule might be. To make the process easier, they began to use certain objects as a trade standard. This revolutionary development was very popular as long as everyone agreed on the object's value and accepted it in trade. In many parts of the world, salt was used as money. It's value and acceptance were nearly universal since it was needed to preserve and flavor food, and was often difficult to find. Other items that were used for early money included tea leaves, shells, feathers, animal teeth, tobacco, blankets and liquor.

In one of the earliest known civilizations, Sumer, barley was used as money. It became apparent, however, that a new form of money that was more manageable was needed. Eventually they began using silver which was hard to find and therefore valuable. The Sumerians melted the silver into small bars and then stamped its exact weight on it. Thus was born the world's first metal money.

The government of Lydia began to use coins and so became the first official money of a government.

Soon the use of silver, copper, and other hard to find objects as money became widespread. In the first century B.C., in what is now Turkey, the government of Lydia began to use coins and so became the first official money of a government. The empires of Greece, Persia and later Rome all devised monetary systems using coins made of gold and silver and copper and bronze. It wasn't until the Middle Ages, however, that paper money was invented. After having traveled to China, Marco Polo returned to Italy in 1295 with the news that the Chinese used paper money. In fact, the Chinese had invented paper as well as a printing process. For hundreds of years, they had been using paper money that was guaranteed by the government to have a certain value.

These forms of money worked quite simply enough because the people who used them trusted that they would. Either the money itself was rare enough or beautiful enough to inspire value, or their king or their government was powerful enough and trustworthy enough to guarantee their value. Had the fundamental understanding of money's value not been accepted, the whole system would have failed — which is the primary reason why Europe was so slow to utilize paper money. Made up of small kingdoms and states that were constantly at war, people had little confidence in their governments. Consequently, it wasn't until Sweden printed paper money in 1661 that the first European country began to use this revolutionary form of money.

By the end of the 16th century the New World had been opened up to the Europeans. In the Americas, Spanish explorers and conquerors mined gold and silver deposits and made them into coins — pieces of eight — which could be cut into smaller pieces called bits. As the Spanish began to expand their power and presence throughout the world, other countries began to adopt Spanish coins as their own currency — often stamping or cutting the coins to show that they were now the official currency of that particular country. The result was that Spanish coins became the most widely used money in the world until the last half of the 19th century.

There were, however, other types of money being used: In the American Pacific Northwest, some coastal tribes used large shield-like copper plates; some Pacific Islanders used feather money consisting of small feathers glued and tied together in coils up to 30 feet long; Yap Islanders used round stones with holes in the middle that were as large as twelve feet across (not surprisingly, it was the world's heaviest money); in Ethiopia, salt was used as money until World War II; Europe created what came to be

After having traveled to China, Marco Polo returned to Italy in 1295 with the news that the Chinese used paper money. In fact, the Chinese had invented paper as well as a printing process.

It wasn't until Sweden printed paper money in 1661 that the first European country began to use this revolutionary form of money.

Yap Islanders used round stones with holes in the middle that were as large as twelve feet across (not surprisingly, it was the world's heaviest money)

"Wampum" was made of shell beads strung together as belts, bracelets and necklaces.

called "manillas" for trade with West African tribes who were fond of horseshoe-shaped metal objects; the Swedes minted platmynt (plate money) in the 17th and 18th centuries. The largest ever circulated, the ten-Daler plate weighed 43 pounds; in America, Virginia and Maryland used tobacco leaves tied into bundles as their official currency during the 17th and 18th centuries; and in 1685, French colonies in Canada printed money in the form of playing cards.

By the 17th century other European countries had established colonies in the New World. In addition to the coinage brought to the Americas by them, there were also systems of money being used by indigenous peoples. "Wampum" was made of shell beads strung together as belts, bracelets and necklaces. Native Americans used this type of money to trade with colonists who, in turn, began to use wampum as money themselves. After the American Revolution in 1776, all the colonies began to mint and print their own money. With the foreign money and the colonies' money all in circulation at the same time, there was quite a lot of confusion when it came to trading. The Continental Congress established a single official currency for the colonies and, in 1787, the first coin was minted: A copper cent stamped with the words "We Are One," and "Mind Your Business." In 1790, the Constitution was ratified and the United States of America officially became a country. Because of the scarceness of precious metal, citizens contributed objects that could be melted down and turned into coins. It's rumored that the first coins minted were actually from George Washington's family silver.

Money systems that are used today were adopted by most countries in the 1800s. In recent years the concept of money has been refined even further so that today we can use checks, credit cards, ATM cards, have bills deducted directly from our banking accounts, and do our banking at home by computer. Still, the primary purpose of money, which is a tool or the means by which a thing or end is accomplished, remains precisely what it was when its concept was adopted by nomads who might well have traded a dozen squirrels and a dozen rabbits for a wild boar.

The arena in which money systems function is called an economy which, understandably, developed along a parallel course with money systems. In fact, one can safely say that where there was a money system, there too was an economy. Broadly defined as a system of producing, distributing and consuming wealth, an economy provides the mechanism whereby a social unit manages its resources. Whether it's a family, a community, state, country or the world, there is a system or organization designed to administer the will of its members and manage the fruits of that will. Needless to say, some systems work better than others on specific issues. If one thinks of an economy as a software program to be installed on computers, one would naturally pick the program that best suits their needs. For instance, one type of economy may be more favorable for an under-developed third world country, while another may be more appropriate for an industrialized country moving toward a more advanced socialization phase. An example of the former would be some of the struggling countries in Africa whose most important and immediate challenges are basic education for its citizens and establishing an acceptable minimum standard of living. An example of the latter would be Russia and some of the former Soviet block countries seeking to incorporate a more productive economic platform into their already established society.

The Continental Congress established a single official currency for the colonies and, in 1787, the first coin was minted: A copper cent stamped with the words "We Are One," and "Mind Your Business."

It's rumored that the first coins minted were actually from George Washington's family silver.

National economies range from closed, government-administered and regulated economies such as those found in many communist countries, and open, laissez faire systems such as those found, to a certain extent, in many democratic countries — although pure forms of each are nonexistent.

An economy provides the mechanism whereby a social unit manages its resources.

Although extensive trade and market expansion began very soon after we as a species began to build permanent dwellings and rely on traveling merchants to provide things that were needed but not immediately available in the vicinity, the evolution of advanced economies can be traced directly to the Industrial Revolution which began essentially in Great Britain in the 18th and 19th centuries. By dramatically increasing the productivity in its economy, it necessitated a more advanced system through which the will of society could be served. With the advent of mechanized production process and the vast increase in production possibilities and profit potential, the need for capital investment to build and buy machines and parts increased substantially. Furthermore, because of the dramatic increase in productivity, new markets had to be developed and others opened up to insure the products being mass produced would have buyers. Consequently, the function of the economy became much more important. As the concept of money as a tool began to show its staggering potential and Western Europe began to build and develop and expand its economic reach, new ideas about how economies should and could best function began to blossom. In 1776, Adam Smith published *The Wealth of Nations*, a study of classical political economies.

As technological advances in travel and communication began to transform the face of Western civilization, and other countries throughout the world began to industrialize, expand current markets and open up new ones where their products might be sold, local economies blossomed international economies. With the development and refinement of electronic communication and international flight in the 20th century that enabled something ordered from London on Tuesday to arrive in New York on Wednesday, the simple economy — a mechanism whereby a social unit manages its resources — had by its own nature blossomed into a global economy.

Today we live in a thriving, bustling global economy. Funds can be transferred electronically in the blink of an eye and products can be shipped half way around the world in less than 24 hours. Computers in department stores in New York are linked to computers in basement studios in Paris, France. Satellites enable live video of an earthquake in Tokyo to be seen in Toledo, and a men's downhill ski race in Aspen to be seen in Lake Geneva. A war in Saudi Arabia drives the price of gas up in Los Angeles; a freak cold snap in Florida causes the price of orange juice in Maine to skyrocket; a great fire in Colombia burns millions of acres of coffee beans, driving the cost of beans through the roof, forcing coffee houses in Seattle to buy their beans from Peru which is invaded by a taste-destroying parasite which causes Seattle coffee drinkers to get sick and when the press gets hold of the story the public is outraged.

Since we have the ability to satisfy our wants and needs with relative ease, and because consumer attitudes and sensibilities are being conditioned to expect it, we can no longer expect to remain unaffected by events in other parts of the world. Our lives are inextricably linked by economics. Where once nationalism and fierce market protections were the rule, now in an international marketplace, cooperation and facilitation rule the day.

Recently in Denver, the seven economic leaders of the free world, and Russia, met to discuss, among

> The evolution of advanced economies can be traced directly to the Industrial Revolution which began essentially in Great Britain in the 18th and 19th centuries.

In 1776, Adam Smith published *The Wealth of Nations*, a study of classical political economies.

Where once nationalism and fierce market protections were the rule, now in an international marketplace, cooperation and facilitation rule the day.

other things, how they can more effectively work together to expand economic possibilities. Some interesting things came out of the historic summit.

A U.S. rocket manufacturing company announced plans to purchase rocket engines from Russia who, just ten years ago, was our arch enemy. Asian and European countries agreed to continue the process of opening up their markets to foreign goods by deregulation. The European Union championed Europe's impending switch to a single currency. The major industrialized countries agreed to rekindle their efforts to spur private investment in Africa. Goals for economic growth were set for major industrialized countries that would be reviewed yearly to determine success and progress.

Though broad in scope and certainly ambitious, the message is clear: expanding economic opportunity is priority one.

Economics is the force that drives progress. Economically, it's apparent that we're headed toward a frontier with infinite possibilities. We've already reached the point where most financial transactions don't even involve cash or coins. The process whereby the concept of tangible money becomes increasingly abstract is perhaps more active now than in any time in history. Not only are we asked to take on faith how much value a particular piece of paper has, we're asked to trust that credit card and bank account numbers communicated electronically to strangers and computers on the other side of the world will be used only by whom and for what they're authorized. With automated shopping for everything from grocery stores to gas pumps, on-line banking and investing . . . can banking on the moon be that far off!

In the last 50 years, the world has undergone dramatic social and political changes. Japan has recovered from catastrophic devastation in World War II and become one of the world's premier economic powerhouses. So too have many European countries. China is experimenting with open markets under a Communist form of government and now, with control of Hong Kong, the economic capital of the Far East, China is poised to bring unprecedented economic firepower to bear on the global marketplace.

Maps made as little as 11 or 12 years ago are no longer valid. And as social change has swept across the face of the globe, so to has economic change. Once closed mega-markets ruled by tyrannical powers are now open to world-wide trade and are ripe for economic development. Russia, one of the most populated countries in the world, is suddenly a fertile hotbed of capitalism. In many of these countries, investment opportunities that existed in the United States 50 years ago are now available. Long suffering, oppressed and stifled citizens are hungry for economic prosperity. And the most fundamental rule of economics is that where there is demand, soon there will be supply.

Economics is the force that drives progress.

The process whereby the concept of tangible money becomes increasingly abstract is perhaps more active now than in any time in history.

And the most fundamental rule of economics is that where there is demand, soon there will be supply.

As the world opens its markets and marketing departments go about their business of creating demand and technology goes about its business of creating supply (not always in that order), it's clear that the economic opportunities on the horizon are virtually infinite. With the move toward a global economy, the need for a strong basic understanding of not only economics, but of different cultures and societies is essential. How the future evolves will be determined by how well we prepare future generations to deal with a global economy.

Maps made as little as 11 or 12 years ago are no longer valid.

How the future evolves will be determined by how well we prepare future generations to deal with a global economy.

There are more than 100 million computers in the world today. The Internet has made the global economy as close as a desk top and as intimate as pointing and clicking. Even the smallest of Mom and Pop companies can now compete with Fortune 500 companies in markets throughout the world. Web pages enable a company with an advertising budget of few hundred dollars a year to compete with companies with an advertising budget of several million dollars.

The Internet has made the global economy as close as a desk top and as intimate as pointing and clicking.

Virtually every industry has already been or will be effected by the computer revolution. Goods and services are now being bought and sold in every country in the world with a simple point and click. New markets are springing up all over the world because of the computer revolution. Issues that hadn't even been dreamed of 20 years ago, except in science fiction, are now being taught and discussed in junior high and high school level courses. Pragmatic studies in international law and finance and commerce and communications are among the most popular majors in colleges and graduate schools all over the world. Foreign companies regularly attend recruiting fairs on college campuses across the country. Companies look for job applicants fluent not only in several languages, but in several computer software languages, as well.

According to Bill Gates, president of Microsoft, the world's most successful software company, there is a massive shift underway in the way people communicate and relate to information. "No one can stop productive change in the long run because the marketplace inexorably embraces it," he says in his book, *The Road Ahead*. And with his track record, I don't know too many people who would take him to task on this observation.

"No one can stop productive change in the long run because the marketplace inexorably embraces it."

— Bill Gates

It's clear that the global economy is already here — and it's not something that only economists and executives from major international companies need to understand. Those of us who have at least a basic understanding of the dynamics of the global marketplace will no doubt have a leg up on those who don't and, consequently, be in position to take advantage of the opportunities that it will bring — assuming, of course, that we have the fundamental financial management skills necessary to do so.

Resources

Books

Eyewitness Books: Money, by Joe Cribb (Knopf). An encyclopedic history of money, foreign currency and trading. (primary or intermediate)

From Gold to Money, by Ali Mitgutsch (Carolrhoda Books). Defines bartering, counterfeiting, minting and earning money. (primary)

Money, by Benjamin Elkin (Children's Press). Explains why we use money and what we can do with it. (primary)

Software

The Coin Changer (Heartsoft). Money-counting and time skills are taught using realistic graphics. (primary)

Money and Time Adventures of the Lollipop Dragon (Society for Visual Education). Lollipop Dragon leads kids through their paces to learn basic money-counting skils. (early primary)

Money Works (MECC). Helps kids learn to recognize values of different coins, buy things, count correct change and see how international exchange rates affect their money's value in other currency systems. (primary)

Banks

Young Americans Bank. Offers savings accounts, checking accounts, credit cards and loans; has mail-in customers from all 50 states and several foreign countries. The average customer is nine years old and has a balance of $260. Write or call for more information: 311 Steele St., Denver, CO 80206; (303) 321-2265.

Chapter 4

The Old Fashioned Way

There was a commercial on television not long ago that featured the accomplished actor John Houseman. He played the part of a senior partner in a venerable investment banking firm who's motto was: " . . . we make money the old fashioned way — we earn it!"

Though this axiom may seem straightforward enough and firmly entrenched in common sense, it may be surprising to find that for a great many people, the wisdom of it is elusive.

As a former stock broker and investment advisor, I've been privy to some amazing stories of financial irresponsibility. A few years ago, I had a client, a fairly young guy, who came to me and said he had some money he wanted to deposit in his account. Though it wasn't a terribly large amount of money — $35,000 — it was somewhat unusual for him to have that much since he wasn't a wealthy man. I asked him if he had inherited it. He answered that he didn't really like to tell people about it, but that he and his brother had won a million dollars in the Colorado Lottery — they shared the ticket.

I asked him if it had changed his life. He responded that he had tried not to let it, that his full year's annuity was what he was depositing in his account.

"I'm going to invest all of it. I'm not going to do what my brother did."

I asked him what his brother had done and he said that his brother had held a better job than he had and made a lot more money. As soon as he won the lottery, he quit his job and started living like a millionaire. He told all of his friends, so naturally when they went out to dinner or out drinking, his friends would inevitably say, "Let Chuck get this one — he's a millionaire."

His brother began acting like a millionaire — taking limousines everywhere he went and spending his money freely and thoughtlessly. Eventually his brother went bankrupt and had to sell his annuity for pennies on the dollar. Unemployed and unhirable, his entire life was fouled up because he had no concept of financial responsibility. When his ship came in, the windfall blew him away.

My client, on the other hand, invested the lion's share of his winnings by buying land and other investments that have increased in value and he plans to retire soon.

Another example of financial irresponsibility happened to a world class athlete — a basketball player from the south side of Chicago. A high school phenomenon, he was highly recruited by almost every major college basketball powerhouse in the country. He enrolled at a perennial national championship caliber university. After two extremely successful years there where he was an All American guard on a final four team, he decided to declare hardship and enter the professional draft after his sophomore year, his reasoning being that, since he was prone to injury (he had blown out his knee in high school), his stellar performance for the last two years in college had made his stock high. Since there was the distinct possibility that he might suffer an injury during his final two years in school, he thought it was best that he go pro as soon as possible so he could cash in on his current value. Taken early in the third round by a "rebuilding" team, he signed a lucrative two-year deal worth a little over a million dollars a year with a healthy signing bonus.

Before even reporting for training camp, he bought a large house with a swimming pool, a Mercedes convertible, a Land Rover, a tricked out Harley Davidson, and a cache of clothes, jewelry and miscellaneous expensive electronic toys that would be the envy of an oil sheik. There were also a couple of expensive junkets to Las Vegas where he dropped what most Americans would consider the equivalent of a year's salary at the black jack table and roulette wheel.

The season rolled around and, as most everyone expected, he saw limited playing time. Unaccustomed to the view of the game from the bench, he became depressed and his gambling habit grew. When the team was on the east coast he frequented Atlantic City; when on the west coast, he was a regular in Las Vegas. When the team found themselves somewhere in between, he always managed to find a high stakes poker or craps game in the town they were in.

As the season wore on and his team struggled to climb out of the division cellar, they decided to unload the disappointing rookie as a "gimmie" in a large seven-player-plus-future-draft-choices trade that brought a couple of tried and true veterans and a "project" rookie center to the team.

Feeling slighted and unwanted and adrift in a new city, the former phenomenon, now a struggling point guard, became even more depressed and his gambling habit, already dangerously out of control, became even worse. Soon his expensive toys and cars were being repossessed by the bank and he had had to take out loans using his expensive property as collateral to cover his ever-escalating gambling debts. It all came to a screeching halt in a play-ground pick-up game he was in (with a wager on the outcome, of course) when he landed awkwardly after a reverse slam dunk and blew out his knee — the healthy uninjured one!

The last anyone heard of the youthful player, he was living a few blocks from where he grew up, drumming up back alley craps games to pay for a heroin habit that sucked the last of his money and his health from him at the ripe age of 23.

Or consider the case of the recent college graduate who used student loans to pay his way through school. Upon graduation, he was inundated with pre-approved credit card applications. Convinced that plastic was a right of passage into adulthood, he applied for several and was, of course, approved. Of course he would need a good suit and nice shoes and all the accessories for job interviews — completely understandable for a young man on the brink of entering the work force. Perhaps even a second suit — after all, you wouldn't want to wear the same suit for a call-back interview. Of course his apartment was furnished in neo-college-dorm-room chic: Cement blocks and two-by-four shelving, with

Convinced that plastic was a right of passage into adulthood, he applied for several and was, of course, approved.

license plates and swimsuit models, and a red naugahyde sofa found next to a dumpster in back of his apartment building as his only piece of furniture. To him it was obvious that he needed a new decor befitting his new status in the world.

Now that there were no more nightly study marathons, there was plenty of time for going out — and certainly a new credit card holder should celebrate his right of passage by buying dinner and a few rounds — during which celebration he happened to meet the most lovely woman in the world who also had expensive tastes. A play and dinner here, a weekend in the mountains there, and before you know it, all his credit cards were maxed — and he still hadn't been offered the career track job he wanted.

Over the three months he'd been celebrating his right of passage into adulthood, he'd taken a temporary job so he could pay his apartment rent and pay some of the expenses, but it was nowhere near enough to cover the collective minimum payment on all his credit cards. Soon he began missing payments — utilities, phone, apartment, and finally his prized credit cards. Within no time, his credit rating was destroyed, he was over his head in debt, and his future looked so bleak that it was all he could do to type up a resume and send it off — let alone conduct himself in actual interviews in a manner that would make someone want to hire him. He ended up getting some financial help from a credit counseling service. Three years later he's still employed by the temp service, albeit in a management position. His credit rating is trashed and he pays cash for everything; but at least he has a girlfriend who would just as soon eat at McDonald's as at Chez René, as long as it's with him.

If any one thing is apparent to me now, it's that people who have earned money before, and who have at least some financial management skills, are far more likely to understand and therefore succeed where financial matters are concerned than those who have simply had those concepts dumped on them. Too often it came in one of those uncomfortable conversations every parent must have with their children and then cross off the list, never to be discussed again. Some learn whatever skills they have by watching their friends or, worse, watching TV. I shudder at the thought of my children learning financial skills from *Melrose Place* or *The Simpsons*.

I shudder at the thought of my children learning financial skills from *Melrose Place* or *The Simpsons*.

Much of our current economic situation can be directly attributed to a profound inattention to the basics of financial management. Americans in particular have assumed an almost providential ownership of economic understanding, due in large part to our own success and the massive socio-political economic marketing. We are programmed to believe that we are economically superior to everyone else in the world. Granted, in the past and, to a certain degree, even now, results tend to support this. Nevertheless, the idea that financial responsibility is an inherent characteristic of our personality is shallow and even dangerous in a world where economics is a matter of life and death.

Much of our current economic situation can be directly attributed to a profound inattention to the basics of financial management.

Simple fundamental skills are never really learned by merely saying something is so and then moving on to the next do-or-don't. Furthermore, while skills may be learned by watching others — parents, friends, television programs, etc. — they are not adequately internalized. The only way real learning happens is when the one learning has a vested, identifiable interest in the learning process and feels a part of the process.

This is why such an emphasis is placed on experiential learning in thoughtful educational environments, and why I advocate an experiential process to teaching kids financial responsibility.

> The only way real learning happens is when the one learning has a vested, identifiable interest in the learning process and feels a part of the process.

Everyone living and breathing on this planet has some form of intellectual infrastructure whereby they process information. Even the most primitive of our ancestors had a kind of intellectual infrastructure (based, of course, on avoiding pain and finding food, etc.). Gradually, more refined systems were developed — each reflecting geographical, political, religious, economic and other factors that weighed on the particular society at the time — until, by processes of social evolution, our current intellectual infrastructure was, over time, "installed." Granted there are many versions and variations and combinations of these intellectual infrastructures. For instance, there are substantial differences between Eastern countries' and Western countries' thought processing, as well as significant differences between third world countries and industrialized nations.

The idea of intellectual infrastructures may be better understood to our culture by viewing it in terms of computers. If you think of it as the software (an educational foundation) that is loaded onto our hardware (our minds), it may be a little easier to understand. When information is collected or otherwise dealt with, it's processed according to the version of the software program that has been installed.

When a child processes the various pieces of information and feedback that accompanies any experience, he or she forms a system by which all future information from endeavors that may be construed as related are processed. With a fundamental experience in financial management, the child will form a system to collect, collate and otherwise process the myriad bits and pieces of information that are generated from that experience. Once arranged within the confines of their newly created system of understanding, the child begins to connect with information that has relevance and expand both the possibilities of and the application of his or her system of organization.

When children manage their own money and assets, they will not only learn the rules of the game, so to speak, but will also familiarize themselves with the playing board — even more when, because of a bad money management decision, children lose money that was to be used on a new pair of Nike sneakers or a Nintendo or a ski trip. If a connection can be made between the rule that the child may have broken, or the hidden hazard on the game board that was overlooked or underestimated, and the loss of money that would have been used for sneakers or computer games or lift tickets, it's almost certain that the same mistake will not be repeated. It's very much like the process of learning that happens when a child sticks his hand on a hot stove.

It's very much like the process of learning that happens when a child sticks his hand on a hot stove.

Moreover, as skills become second nature and the offshoot of those skills reinforce ideals and help develop values, the child begins to develop a voice that has significance and meaning — an important psycho-social development that strengthens self-esteem and self-worth. Quite simply, earning money not only provides monetary rewards and life options and choices, it also provides experiences that build character and instill values.

One of the best ways to begin the process of experiential training is to introduce children to the concept of earning money. Not only will they begin to develop a sense of both concrete and abstract value and learn about some basic principles of money management, but they will also have a springboard for learning more advanced concepts that will allow them to see how money can make its own money — an important skill to have in our current socio-economic environment, and a necessity for the future.

In a capitalist economy where so much of our personality revolves around the idea of making money, it's inevitable that a certain amount of our self (and social) esteem hangs in the balance. Child psychologists say that many of the personality problems children have stem from a lack of self-esteem. And from that, many other personality disorders may arise. With the confidence that comes from successfully managing one's own finances, many self-esteem problems may be avoided and, in fact, can increase a child's self-esteem at a very important and difficult time in his or her life — a point when many kids turn to anti-social behavior in hopes of gaining acceptance among their peers. Renowned psychologist Jean Piaget says that children need positive experiences for cognitive development, and to attain certain levels of competence and understanding in order to advance to the next developmental stage. When these experiences don't happen, the ability of a child to develop and integrate life experiences for use in adulthood is compromised, perhaps even damaged, in the same way that someone who has been denied nutritious food in order to develop physically will not grow properly or, in many cases, begin to deteriorate physically.

Granted, there are a great many other things that children need for a healthy sense of self-worth. But the fact remains, an educational activity that introduces children to productive principles is a positive experience that empowers children at an important time in their lives, and gives them skills that can do the same as they grow into adulthood.

The idea of earning money has been instrumental in the development not only of individuals, but of societies as well — ours in particular. Our collective personality has been shaped by an almost providential mandate to make money. As much as any other single contributing factor, the idea of sustaining and improving our lot in life has driven us to great heights as far as achievements — both pecuniary and philosophically. It is, after all, at the very core of the American dream.

> Our collective personality has been shaped by an almost providential mandate to make money.

The same basic laws of development that hold true for individuals also hold true for society.

When advanced societies neglect basic social needs, the consequences can be severe — even terminal.

Throughout history, societies that have excelled economically have also excelled in other just as important arenas such as the arts, sciences, philosophy, and others. The same basic laws of development that hold true for individuals also hold true for society. Before a society can move on to more advanced and fulfilling pursuits, basic needs must be satisfied. We see this regularly in developing countries: economic growth is dependent upon satisfying primary needs like a stable currency, a reliable infrastructure, a certain level of trade and commerce, making sure its citizens are not starving, etc. After these things have been accomplished, a country may be able to turn its attention to more advanced issues and causes, like economic growth and development, facilitating domestic capital investment, wooing foreign capital investment, social reform, etc. Certainly this was the case when unhappy British citizens began to settle what would one day become the United States. Two hundred years or so later, we even went so far as to name a political philosophy "The Great Society."

The inverse of this is also true: when advanced societies neglect basic social needs, the consequences can be severe — even terminal. We've seen this time and time again throughout history — both in ancient times, as in Rome and Greece, and recently, as in the breakup of the former Soviet Union and its satellite countries where neglect of basic economic issues and principles spelled disaster for "great societies."

The simple fact of the matter is that economic growth and development is essential for both an individual and a society if they are to transcend elemental circumstances to take advantage of opportunities that satisfy more sophisticated and advanced needs. And if the axiom that a whole is only as good as it parts is true, it's absolutely necessary that basic financial management skills be taught at an early age so that children can take advantage of the opportunities that await them.

It's extremely important that our children learn the fundamentals of money management at as early an age as possible. Both seasoned parents and psychologists alike insist that the purest form of learning is experiential. This type of learning is perhaps more important and effective now than in any point in history since so many seductive alternative ways to do things exist.

On the other hand, when you actually do a particular thing, you're much more likely to learn the various elements involved since the results — whether good or bad — are strong reinforcement (positive and negative) for what you've done and, whether you're conscious of it or not, will imprint on the personality and create a reference point that will serve as a foundation for the entire learning process.

It doesn't take a mystic to see that the next millennium is approaching like an economic time bomb. Money has and always will be one of the most important tools in building our world — a world that progress changes almost daily. Imagine the leap imaginations have had to make over the last 50 years to accommodate human achievements. In a state of virtual technology that seems only to be gaining steam, it's likely that the future 50 years from now hasn't even been dreamt of yet. It's only common sense that to participate in what is sure to be a complicated world that doesn't even exist yet, a solid and pragmatic foundation for success needs to be built

> It doesn't take a mystic to see that the next millennium is approaching like an economic time bomb.

that will enable and empower the next and future generations to take advantage of the opportunities that will surely await those who understand how to. And there is no better way to learn how to do something than to actually do it.

Resources

Books

Arthur's Funny Money, by Lillian Hoban (Harper and Row). Arthur sets up a bike-washing business to earn money for a T-shirt. (primary)

The Go-Around Dollar, by Barbara Johnston Adams (Four WInds Press). Follows the life of a dollar bill as it travels from person to person. Also explains where and how money is made. (primary)

The Kids Money Book, by Neale S. Godfrey (Checkerboard Press). Answers such questions as: What is a checking account? Where did piggy banks get their name? And how do banks earn their money? (primary and intermediate)

Making Cents: Every Kid's Guide to Money, by Elizabeth Wilkinson (Little, Brown). Offers detailed money-making ideas for older kids. (intermediate)

Your 1st Book of Wealth, by A. David Silver (The Career Press). A beginner's guide to collecting, investing and starting your own business. (teens)

Better Than a Lemonade Stand, by Daryl Bernstein (Beyond Words Publishing). Describes 51 businesses, with hints on which supplies and how much time you'll need, what to charge, how to advertise.

Fast Cash for Kids, by Bonnie and Noel Drew (Career Press). Lists 101 money-making projects for children under 16, arranged by season of the year.

Also includes age-appropriate tips on how to handle the financial end of the business.

The Teenage Entrepreneur's Guide, by Sarah L. Riehm (Surrey Books). Money-making ideas for older teens, and detailed information on preparing a business plan, setting up a bookkeeping system and paying taxes.

A Teen's Guide to Business, by Linda Menzies, Oren S. Jenkins and Rickell R. Fisher. Offers anecdotes from successful teen entrepreneurs and includes a section on how to land a job working for someone else.

The Lemonade Stand: A Guide to Encouraging the Entrepreneur in Your Child, by Emmanuel Modu (Bob Adams, Inc.). A comprehensive guide for parents that includes chapters on legal and tax issues, business ethics, and business concepts your kids should know.

Start Your Own Lemonade Stand, by Steven Caney (Workman Publishing). Do-it-yourself kit with apron, lemon juicer and recipes, plus a booklet with strategies for success.

Periodicals

Ump's Fwat: An Annual Report for Young People (The Acadamy for Economic Education, 125 NationsBank Center, Richmond, VA 23277). A fanciful look at Ump, the first caveman capitalist, that will help kids understand such terms as stockholder and dividend.

Square One: The Newsletter for the Beginning Investor, edited by Amy T. Rauch-Bank ($29.95 per year; 259 Peninsula Lake Dr., Highland, MI 48357).

Software

Hot Dog Stand (Sunburst Communications). Players manage and run a business while operating a hot dog stand at eight computerized football games. The series also includes *Travel Agent Contest, Smart Shopper Marathon* and *Foreman's Assistant.* (intermediate and teens)

Whatsit Corp. (Sunburst Communications). Would-be entrepreneurs run a small, one-product (whats-its) business for six months, making all the same decisions that any business owner must make.

Organizations and Clubs

The Center for Entrepreneurship offers a variety of resources and educational opportunities for prospective entrepreneurs, including students. For more information, write or call the Center for Entrepreneurship, Wichita State University, 1845 N. Fairmount, Wichita, KS 67260; (316) 689-3000.

Kits

The Busines$ Kit is a package of manuals, tapes stationery and other tools designed to teach kids ages 10 to 18 how to start and run a business; includes access to a toll-free hotline that kids can call for advice on business problems. The cost is $49.95, plus $8.95

for postage and handling. For information, call (800) 282-5437.

Part II

A Clean Break

Chapter 5

What You Don't Know . . .

Over the years I've fielded quite a few questions on the subject of teaching kids financial responsibility, ranging from thoughtfully insightful, "Isn't teaching children about money management at such an early age placing too much emphasis on money and encouraging materialism?" to the truly absurd, "Should I charge my 5-year-old son rent so that he'll get a better idea of what the real world is like?" to the simply misinformed, "Isn't it against the law for underaged children to make money?"

Despite the laissez faire way in which the subject is frequently handled by well-intentioned parents, money management skills are not encoded in the DNA of a "wealthy" gene, nor do they blossom at the recitation of a secret magical incantation passed down from one generation to another. It's unlikely that children have acquired fundamentally sound money management skills simply by observing others. Many parents assume that since their children get an allowance, learn about earning money through chores around the house, can make change when someone asks, or perhaps save a little money in their piggy banks, even loan a brother or sister money that's to be repaid in a few days along with two candy bars in interest, that they're learning fine money management skills. And it may be that some of those transactions do indeed promote learning. But to assume that they're learning sound money management principles and financial responsibility is naive even if they have a slightly more enlightened idea about where money comes from than the tooth fairy and even if they've got a good handle on simple financial transactions. No matter how confusing the financial landscape may get in the future and how severely they're ideals may be tested, it may do them a disservice if they're not taking these things to heart and forming a foundational value that remains intact.

The truth is that money management skills must be imprinted on a child's personality in much the same way values are imprinted. Granted, this is an unorthodox way to view something that has for so long been viewed as a right of passage, something that is simply "developed" over time out of need, much like learning to walk or to feed yourself. Elevating financial responsibility to the same psycho-social development level as honesty and trustworthiness and humility, and using the same pragmatic experiential teaching methods that one might use to teach a child how to ride a bicycle (that is to just do it), may seem simple and straightforward enough — and even the natural, logical way to address the issue. But you'd be surprised how many people don't understand the difference that such an approach represents.

Here are some additional questions I'm frequently asked about money management:

> The truth is that money management skills must be imprinted on a child's personality in much the same way values are imprinted.

Q: Wouldn't placing so much emphasis on money and financial skills at an early age risk turning my child into either a miser or spendthrift?

A: Not at all. First of all, you're not placing the emphasis on money and financial skills; you're stressing the importance of self-reliance by teaching sound money management skills in the context of a more financially responsible view of the world you live in. Life management is what we're ultimately emphasizing here — the idea that a person who is able to manage his or her own financial affairs responsibly will be better able to responsibly manage other important areas of life like education and career and family and, perhaps what it all boils down to, time. What we're trying to establish is a more productive and responsible way of thinking about financial matters.

Like a software program for your computer, we're establishing a philosophy by which a child may operate when it comes to financial matters.

> What we're trying to establish is a more productive and responsible way of thinking about financial matters.

Second, we're not establishing a model for getting rich. There are literally hundreds of books and tapes and seminars designed to do that. What we're here concerned with is trying to establish financial responsibility as a value — a way of thinking and a system of organizing information. As I've mentioned, like a software program for your computer, we're establishing a philosophy by which a child may operate when it comes to financial matters.

Q: My 12-year-old has already developed the most irresponsible habits when it comes to handling his money. Is it too late to instill values like financial responsibility in him?

A: There are special difficulties when it comes to teaching older children new habits. The key is to allow the child — and it's the same for any age — to actually experience the results of his or her own decisions so that it becomes imprinted on their personality.

> The key is to allow the child — and it's the same for any age — to actually experience the results of his or her own decisions so that it becomes imprinted on their personality.

As with any conditioned learning, reinforcement strengthens connections. If a child squanders allowance or some other income and doesn't have any money left to go to the big concert that all his friends are going to, he'll be inclined to remember the experience and, if he's smart, adjust his behavior so it doesn't happen again. The reverse is also true; if a child is intent upon a certain item — say a new pair of $100 Nike sneakers — and knows that to get them he must save X amount of his allowance each week, when finally he has enough, the cool new light-as-air sneakers that are the envy of all his friends will be extremely strong reinforcement of the ideals you're trying to impress upon him.

As with any conditioned learning, reinforcement strengthens connections.

Q: My children are experts at weaseling money out of me. They spend their allowance and then see something they want and manipulate me to get it. How can I stop this cycle?

A: Simple. Just stop. In the context of the Four-Part Money Management System introduced in Part III, the parameters are well-established beforehand and everyone know the rules. If for some reason your child comes up short at the end of the week or month and needs more money to go to the movies . . . that's life — really! And the sooner they learn that the better.

Q: My son has absolutely no interest in money or financial issues. How can I interest him in financial responsibility?

A: Probably the best way to interest unenthusiastic children in financial responsibility is to explain to them that someone has to pay for that new snowboard — and it isn't going to be you. Often older children have already begun to form opinions and ideas about financial issues and what's important to them. In these cases, it's necessary to explain to them that things are going to be different from now on, that they will have to learn to manage their own finances so that they can buy the things they want with their own money.

Q: My wife and I are both professionals and work over 60 hours a week. We barely have time to balance our own checkbooks; how can we set aside time to teach our seven and eight year-olds about money management?

If for some reason your child comes up short at the end of the week or month and needs more money to go to the movies . . . that's life — really!

A: You will need to sit down with your children in order to explain what you're doing and why. However, the Four-Part Money Management System is organized in such a way that, once the basic elements and rules have been explained, the rest is up to them. The whole idea behind the financial management model I propose is to let kids do it themselves and learn from their successes and failures. Certainly you will want to point them in the right direction from time to time, but ultimately it's their responsibility to manage their own finances and learn what they can to be more successful. And in the long run (and even in the short run, for that matter — if it's done correctly, of course), you'll be saving yourself time and worry by turning the responsibility over to them.

Q: My children own several different stocks and mutual funds. When the checks come, should the kids be allowed to spend it?

A: No. If you're investing and those investments have rewards to them such as dividends and interest payments, then that money should be reinvested back into the same company or into other companies so that it grows and accumulates. Otherwise, if you keep bleeding the investment for its earnings, it will never have a chance to grow and be worth substantial amounts later on.

> The whole idea behind the financial management model I propose is to let kids do it themselves and learn from their successes and failures.

I cover the issues raised by these questions, and a lot more, in depth in later chapters. Most are easily answered with a little patience, understanding and common sense. The key to successfully teaching children money management skills and financial responsibility is to show them how these things can improve their circumstances now and in the future. If that connection can be solidified and the idea instilled in their personality, the rest is a matter of interpreting experience, processing information, and internalizing lessons.

Maybe It's Me?

One of the things that can effect how children react to instruction in financial responsibility is how they perceive their parents' attitudes toward financial responsibility. If, for instance, children see their parents literally toss cash around the house — onto the dresser or coffee table at night when they come home from work and change clothes — or speak flippantly about the cost of something like an unconcerned scoff at the prospect of buying something not on sale, there's a good chance that they will have the same careless or flippant attitude to financial responsibility that they see in their parents.

It's important that children see genuine concern in their parents' attitude toward whatever they're teaching them — whether it's financial management or study habits or personal hygiene.

It's important that children see genuine concern in their parents' attitude toward whatever they're teaching them — whether it's financial management or study habits or personal hygiene.

Otherwise, it's likely that their commitment to financial education will go the same way as their commitment to good grades or brushing their teeth before they go to bed or making their beds in the morning.

Following is a Parents' Financial Personality Quiz that should help you gauge your own attitude toward financial responsibility, and how well you may be prepared to introduce the concept to your children.

1) Does money occupy your thoughts most of the time?

Yes _____   No _____

2) Do you receive great pleasure watching your financial assets increase?

Yes _____   No _____

3) If you were to come into a large sum of money overnight, would you save most of it?

Yes _____   No _____

4) Would you invest most of it?

Yes _____   No _____

5) Would you spend most of it?

Yes _____   No _____

6) Do you frequently max your credit to the limit?

Yes _____   No _____

7) Are you always in debt at the end of the month?

Yes _____   No _____

8) Is buying the popular things important to you?

Yes _____   No _____

9) Are you envious of your friends who are more comfortable financially?
Yes _____   No _____

10) Do you feel empowered by having money?
Yes _____   No _____

11) Do you worry that you will have no money in your old age?
Yes _____   No _____

12) Do you find it difficult to make decisions about spending money?
Yes _____   No _____

13) Do you usually say you can't afford it when your spouse wants to buy something?
Yes _____   No _____

14) Do you usually know how much money is in your purse or wallet at any given time?
Yes _____   No _____

15) Do you reward yourself with shopping?
Yes _____   No _____

16) Do you frequently buy yourself things to put yourself in a better mood?
Yes _____   No _____

**Scoring for Parent's Financial Personality Quiz:
"Yes" to questions 1, 2, 3, 4, 10, 11, 12, 13 and 14 indicates you have a "saver" type of personality.
"Yes" to questions 5, 6, 7, 8, 9, 15 and 16 indicates you have a "spender" type of personality.**

The Test

One of the things that I hear most often from parents is that they're not really sure how much they themselves know about financial management, not to mention how capable they are of teaching their children. In fact, most parents believe their children already have a fairly good handle on basic financial management skills through the scant instruction they've already given them, and from simply being around when they pay the bills and discuss family financial matters — at least enough to get them by until they take accounting or finance courses in school. Even those parents who have tried to teach their children at least rudimentary financial management skills are not really sure if they're doing it right, or even if they're teaching the right things.

Here's a quick test that should help you evaluate your money management IQ and determine whether you're on the right track with your children's financial education.

1) Do you give your child an allowance?
 ____ A: Yes
 ____ B: No
 ____ C: Sometimes
 ____ D: Only when he/she is good

2) How do you decide how much allowance to give?
 ____ A: Base it on their age
 ____ B: Based upon how I feel
 ____ C: They ask for a certain amount
 ____ D: They get whatever is under the sofa cushions or left in the clothes dryer

Even those parents who have tried to teach their children at least rudimentary financial management skills are not really sure if they're doing it right, or even if they're teaching the right things.

3) How often do you give allowances?

    ___ A: Daily
    ___ B: Weekly
    ___ C: Monthly
    ___ D: Irregularly

4) How much of his/her allowance does your child spend?

    ___ A: None
    ___ B: 10%
    ___ C: 1/3
    ___ D: All of it

5) How much of his/her allowance does your child give?

    ___ A: None
    ___ B: 10%
    ___ C: 1/3
    ___ D: All of it

6) How much of his/her allowance does your child save?

    ___ A: None
    ___ B: 10%
    ___ C: 1/3
    ___ D: All of it

7) How much of his/her allowance does your child invest?

    ___ A: None
    ___ B: 10%
    ___ C: 1/3
    ___ D: All of it

8) Does your son/daughter own any stocks?
___ Yes
___ No

9) Does your son/daughter own any bonds?
___ Yes
___ No

10) Does your son/daughter own any mutual funds?
___ Yes
___ No

11) Does your son/daughter have any bank accounts?
___ Yes
___ No

12) Where does he/she keep his/her money?
___ A: Sock drawer
___ B: Jar
___ C: Piggy Bank
___ D: Allowance Kit
___ E: Bottom of the washing machine

13) How often does your son/daughter ask for more than their allowance?
___ A: Daily
___ B: Rarely
___ C: Constantly
___ D: I don't listen

14) Does he/she do chores?
___ Yes
___ No

15) Are chores tied to his/her allowance?
___ Yes
___ No

16) Do you feel like money is a problem?
   ___ Yes
   ___ No

17) Does he/she do odd jobs to earn extra money?
   ___ Yes
   ___ No

If you and your children are already doing the majority of the things in the preceding test, you're well on your way to teaching your child a sound philosophy of financial responsibility and the fundamentals of money management. If not, it's time to start.

The following chapters in this section will discuss some specific issues that parents and kids face when it comes to money management, and explore some ways in which both parents and children might address those issues.

Resources

Books

Kiplinger's Money Smart Kids (And Parents, Too!), by Janet Bodnar (1993, Kiplinger Books).

The Monster Money Book, Loreen Leedy (Holiday House). Members of the Monster Club discuss money, how to manage and spend their dues and how to be a smart shopper. (primary)

Games

The Allowance Game. A board game where kids travel around the board and encounter ways to spend their allowance, the first player to save $20 wins. For more information, contact: Lakeshore Learning Materials, 2695 E. Dominguez St., Carson, CA 90749; (800) 421-5354; $14.95 plus shipping and hadling. (primary level)

The Reward Game. Players buy and sell stocks, bonds, gold and real estate, the prices of which fluctuate with inflation (real estate and gold go up in price when inflation rises; stocks and bonds go up when inflation falls). You can borrow assets, but the first player to earn $10 million debt-free wins. $35 plus $5 for shipping. The Center's Money-Book Store catalog lists other financial games and books and is available for $1. For more information contact: The National Center for Financial Education; P.O. Box 34070, San Diego, CA 92163; (619) 232-8811. (intermediate and teens)

Chapter 6

We All Make Mistakes

One of the most important characteristics of humankind is our unique ability to make mistakes and learn from them. Indeed, civilization owes a great deal to learning by trial and error. Had it not been for this unique, built-in feature, there's little doubt we'd not have survived as a species. The same holds true for money management. Had it not been for mistakes that, while painful at the time, served as lessons for the future, it's unlikely that any of us — individually or collectively — would have attained even a minimal level of financial stability — much less flourish in an economically progressive culture and society.

Over the years I've been witness to a great many mistakes when it comes to financial matters. I've always been very conscious of those mistakes that confirm our profound general inattention to basic and fundamental financial management principles. As an investment advisor, I've prided myself on being able to put together an investment portfolio for my clients that maximizes earnings and minimizes risk — finding the right combination of financial options, and the right strategies. I can't, however, guard against mistakes that are made because my clients lack a fundamental philosophy of financial responsibility. No matter how well I do my job, a sudden craving for a sports car that goes from zero to 100 in a second and a client who never learned the concept of delayed gratification is a mistake waiting to happen.

No matter how well I do my job, a sudden craving for a sports car that goes from zero to 100 in a second and a client who never learned the concept of delayed gratification is a mistake waiting to happen.

For the most part, mistakes in how we manage our money are obvious and easily traced; it doesn't take a mysterious voice in an underground parking garage to mumble "follow the money." A quick analysis of the point where one's fortunes turned south will almost always reveal a mistake. There are times when mistakes are not so easily recognized, and the lesson to be learned from the experience is delayed. In such cases, the mistakes probably have more to do with values and priorities than with specific financial and economic notions. It's these types of mistakes that we need to address if we're to continue to survive and flourish as individuals and a society.

It's unlikely that one would grasp advanced geometric concepts if at first one was unable to understand what Pythagoras said about triangles, or even worse, imposed an incorrect assumption into the theory simply because they couldn't understand the original correct assumption.

Following Through

Among the most insidious of mistakes are those that have to do with parents' inability or unwillingness to stick with a policy or system that they have decided upon and, consequently, fail to reinforce various elements of that policy or system. This results inevitably in a botched educational experience that is neither enlightened nor useful. What generally happens in such cases is that kids will retain bits and pieces of a haphazardly taught ideal — usually bits and pieces that have a particularly attractive though not necessarily helpful importance, like the piece of the system regarding study habits that says to reward yourself with frequent breaks during study — and mix it with other similarly suspiciously learned ideals. Ultimately they construct something that in no way resembles what the parents had in mind, and may well be detrimental to their prospects for future learning. It's unlikely that one would grasp advanced geometric concepts if at first one was unable to understand what Pythagoras said about triangles, or even worse, imposed an incorrect assumption into the theory simply because they couldn't understand the original correct assumption. I certainly wouldn't want to travel across the bridge that this architect designed if by some fluke he happened to finagle his way through school and into a job. It's extremely important for parents to follow through with the teaching process by both sticking with their part of the deal, thus reinforcing what they're teaching.

One of the most common mistakes of this type is parents who set up an allowance system but fail to allot the agreed upon sum on the agreed upon day. Such an arbitrary arrangement will invariably cause children to discount the seriousness of not only the allowance system itself, but of their parents' commitment to the underlying ideal. It's difficult to teach a child the parameters of money management if those parameters are arbitrary. Understanding money management without a reliable source of income is nothing if not an exercise in futility. Often kids will further illustrate the nature of the original mistake by appealing to their parents for unscheduled money for spur of the moment purchases, claiming that if their parents had given them their allowance when they were supposed to, they wouldn't have to ask now.

Understanding money management without a reliable source of income is nothing if not an exercise in futility.

Advances on Allowances

Which raises another issue that frequently causes problems when trying to instill financial responsibility in kids: giving advances on allowances. By discarding set rules and caving in to unscheduled money requests, parents again belittle the ideal they're trying to teach and, in the process, teach children that even if they spend foolishly or otherwise manage their money unwisely, it's O.K. since, apparently from their example or precedent, there is an unlimited supply for the asking and, by implication, that it's not so important to manage your money well. Another implication of giving advances on allowances is that the concept of delayed gratification is all but lost. One of the primary goals of any system of money management is to teach through experience the importance and necessity of planning and budgeting so that one has enough money to purchase the things one wants and needs. If children begin to learn that they can have anything they want — even if they can't afford it — by simply asking their parents for more, there's little incentive for them to manage their money responsibly. It's not a wild prediction to say that such children will likely grow up using the immediate purchasing power of credit cards as a substitute for parents to squelch the pangs and growls of immediate gratification.

Credit and Debt

Another trouble area that I've seen all too often is introducing kids to debt before they can appreciate its dangers and advantages.

Another trouble area that I've seen all too often is introducing kids to debt before they can appreciate its dangers and advantages. With the impression that their children will learn the issues involved in credit and get used to interest and monthly payments and such, most parents see it as an opportunity to show their children what life is like in their world. Unfortunately, children rarely internalize the educational aspects and instead focus on the fact that they can be immediately gratified without having any money. The reality of the situation is that children learn bad habits and develop behaviors that, quite frankly, are detrimental to financial responsibility. More than likely, these children will grow up with the idea that buying things on credit is just fine — after all, their parents are the ones who suggested it years ago. And certainly they wouldn't advocate something that is not good.

Instead of introducing credit to kids at such an early age — and for items that decrease in value by half as soon as you walk out of the store with them — wait until they're old enough to understand that buying something on credit can be the best way to go if what you're purchasing can be seen as an investment. Loans for their college education may be the best introduction to credit that a child can have since it will not only introduce them to loans and interest, but it will be a good lesson in investments. In a perfect world, it might even contribute to a greater appreciation of college, hopefully motivating them to attend the classes they enroll in since they are paying for it — and will continue paying for several years after college, for that matter.

Budgets

Another area where mistakes are frequently made is budgets. The problem is that drawing up a budget before you understand the dynamics of budgeting is like drawing a set of plans for a house without understanding how it's built. The inevitable failure to meet the requirements of a budget that is drawn up in this situation is enough to dash the enthusiasm and motivation of most adults. For kids it can be fatal to their financial education.

The best way to introduce them to budgeting is to get them started without it. When the results of their financial decisions begin to register, both good and bad, they'll be able to see the various factors that effect financial management such as interest rates and service charges and the like. They'll also be able to gauge their own ability and conviction to keep their hands off savings no matter how badly they want that new snowboard or the coolest blouse ever in the history of the world. Once they get a feel for the different factors that effect the budgeting process, and their own stick-to-it-tiveness, then it will be time to introduce the concept of budgets to them. The

The positive reinforcement that comes from successfully budgeting their finances will be one of the strongest connections they ever make in financial management.

After all, life itself is a trial and error process; why should anyone expect financial management and responsibility to be anything different?

positive reinforcement that comes from successfully budgeting their finances will be one of the strongest connections they ever make in financial management. And from that time on, they'll have the confidence to write their own ticket, so to speak.

On the other hand, a failed attempt at budgeting can make a child so disenchanted with financial management, and with their own abilities, that ultimately they'll lose confidence in themselves and interest in financial management and never understand its benefits. After all, who among us hasn't come home from work so tired that cooking seemed like a major production, and ended up ordering out a pizza or Chinese "just this once" so often that very soon, the household expenses budget is completely blown? I'd venture to guess that very few of us renewed our commitment and tried it again. Most likely we just gave up budgeting household expenses because the anxiety and self-loathing that we inevitably felt was much too intense to ever put ourselves through again. Such a feeling can be absolutely disastrous for children just beginning to develop their personality and sense of self-worth.

The best way to introduce children to budgets is to let them make enough mistakes that they can see for themselves how better organized money management would have helped in a particular situation. After all, life itself is a trial and error process; why should anyone expect financial management and responsibility to be anything different?

Ducking the Issue

In many families, discussion of financial matters is something that is avoided like the plague. Often money is a taboo subject for a variety of reasons.

Many times it's avoided because it is an embarrassing topic. I've had clients in the past who came to see me about beginning a financial portfolio. When I asked them about their financial status and what they hoped to achieve, it was like pulling teeth to get information from them. Many times family finances is something that just isn't discussed — especially around the children. As we all know, when someone brings up a topic that gets awkward glances and silences, it only makes the topic that much more mysterious. I've even had a client whose wife didn't know how much money he made.

Financial matters shouldn't be relegated to the same status as skeletons in the closet.

Resources

Books

The Berenstain Bears Get the Gimmies, by Stan and Jan Berenstain (Random House). Brother and Sister Bear come down with a case of the "galloping, greedy gimmies." Other money-oriented books in this popular series include *Trouble With Money*, *Mama's New Job*, *Meet Santa Bear*. (primary)

Every Kid's Guide to Intelligent Spending, by Joy Berry (Living Skills Press). Teaches children about advertising, impulse spending and how to be a thoughtful consumer. Berry has also written *Every Kid's Guide to Making and Managing Money*. (primary)

The Money Book: A Smart Kid's Guide to Savvy Saving and Spending, by Elaine Wyatt and Stan Hinden (Tambourine Books). Tips and hints about earning, banking, budgeting and saving money. (primary)

Smart Spending: A Young Consumer's Guide, by Lois Schmitt (Charles Scribner's Sons). Explores budgeting, misleading advertising, consumer fraud, warranties and consumer complaints. (teens)

Chapter 7

Breaking Old Habits

One of the most damaging mistakes one can make when trying to instill basic principles of financial responsibility in children is also one of the most common: Allowing old habits to persist. This is a failing we can all identify with to some extent. You purchase a coffee table and, determined to keep it free of water rings, scratches and stains, you pledge to never again eat in the living room while watching TV; or you promise yourself never to use the automatic car wash on your brand new car; or maybe, determined to spend more time with your family, you vow to never again to bring work home. But as surely and certainly as bills come due, you find yourself doing a little double-checking of facts and figures, a little early meeting preparation, some weekend proposal revisions for a Monday morning staff meeting, and before you know it, the old nemesis is staring you right in the face. Again there's no time for that family camping trip or the piano recital or even the round of golf that you've been planning for the last six weeks. After a while, the available time you do have at home is hardly quality time since you're tired from all the work-related projects and deadlines hanging over your head, and you're moody because you're resolutions have fallen by the wayside.

Teaching a basic philosophy of financial responsibility is no different. The underlying reason to do so in the first place is to break the cycle of poor money management that, for the most part, is the result of too much "monkey see, monkey do."

The underlying reason to do so in the first place is to break the cycle of poor money management that, for the most part, is the result of too much "monkey see, monkey do."

When it comes to teaching money management skills to your children, if you're like most parents, you've been doing things a certain way for quite a long time and probably learned your skills from watching your parents or friends or maybe from a few courses or an occasional article. Despite knowing that much of what you're teaching your kids could be handled better — perhaps even needs to be rethought and completely overhauled — you assume they'll refine their skills when they get older or, hopefully, will marry well. And anyhow, there are more important things to be teaching your children than money management skills, aren't there?

Maybe you know adults who lack the fundamental skills to be self-sufficient. You've seen your next door neighbors take out a second mortgage on their home to pay for three years of college because their 18-year-old spent the entire amount they'd saved for four years of college in her first year. Maybe a friend's eight-year-old son has been double-whammied by the world's greatest basketball player whose latest commercial promotes a pair of magical sneakers that will enable him to do a 360 degree slam dunk as soon as he laces them up. He insists that his parents buy them for him immediately so he can be a star player. Of course he promises to reimburse them many times over once he signs the gazillion-dollar NBA contract that the commercial promised him was his if he wore the sneakers. On the other hand, maybe you've come to the realization that your child's future self-sufficiency is in jeopardy right in your own home when she asks you innocently for another $10 to replace the $10 you gave her yesterday which she lost — apparently as effortlessly as if she'd lost a hair barrette or a button or, the way you thought of it, a penny.

If at first it seems like the money management behaviors that your children have developed are far too ingrained and, consequently, trying to change them would be like trying to teach a dog not to bark, take heart: dog psychologists insist that barking is a simple habit and have had a good deal of success in breaking that habit — even in older dogs who, as everyone knows, are not easily given to new tricks.

The only way to effectively break old habits is to break cleanly from them and in no uncertain terms. First and foremost, everyone in the family needs to sit down and discuss exactly what it is that they hope to accomplish by instilling fundamental principles of financial responsibility. What are the goals of such an undertaking? How will it be different from the

> The only way to effectively break old habits is to break cleanly from them and in no uncertain terms.

way things are done now? How will it effect the lives of those involved? What will be expected as far as commitment is concerned? For you, the parents? For your children? Only after goals are clearly and simply defined and related issues are discussed is it time for a clean break from the old in favor of the new. Then you can lay down the new system:

1) You're going to get an allowance. You're getting an allowance because you are a member of this family;

2) You're going to manage that allowance correctly. In other words, you need to show that you're going to handle your allowance properly, and we're going to show you how to do that with spending, giving, saving, and investing;

3) You are also going to be given a set of chores that you are responsible for, not because you're paid to do them, but because you are a member of this family.

We've all known people — friends, relatives, even ourselves — who are never quite able to leave the baggage of former relationships out of new, potentially successful relationships. No matter how much effort is taken to begin anew, sometimes residue from the past seeps into the present; and if it goes unrecognized and unaddressed for long enough, into the future. Invariably relationships that evolve in such a situation are marked by confusion and miscommunication and, inevitably, end miserably, which only adds to the amount of baggage that is brought into the next relationship. Unless, of course, lessons are learned. And perhaps most important of all is the lesson that says anything new will quickly become old if a clean break isn't made. It is, after

No matter how much effort is taken to begin anew, sometimes residue from the past seeps into the present; and if it goes unrecognized and unaddressed for long enough, into the future.

all, pointless to start something new if your thinking is mired in the old, in the way you use to do things. It's like a gaudy gift that gets passed on time and time again. True, the wrapping paper is different each time it's opened, but once opened, the glow of excitement and anticipation gives way to forced smiles hiding disappointment. It's still the same old gaudy gift.

Of course children can't be expected to exercise the same amount of restraint and forward thinking as adults. And here is where parents must accept the responsibility of involvement in not only initial instruction and education, but in the ongoing process as well. Central to the system I propose is that children learn from their mistakes, but it's unrealistic to ask parents to stand by while they watch their children do something that is painful and quite possibly destructive. Therein lies the nature of the job of parenting — when to intervene to save a child from pain, and when to stand back and allow the situation and circumstances to do the teaching.

Therein lies the nature of the job of parenting — when to intervene to save a child from pain, and when to stand back and allow the situation and circumstances to do the teaching.

Therefore, it's incumbent upon parents to be involved with their children's financial education by staying on top of the situation, and wherever prudent, helping them avoid mistakes before they happen. This may be in the form of giving them information, or showing them where to get information for themselves, so that they can make their own informed decision more responsibly. It can take the form of encouraging them in a certain direction, or at times even prohibiting them from something that you know is wrong.

Another way parents need to stay involved with their children's financial education to ensure that old habits don't seep in, is to make certain parents hold up their end. If parents fall back into old habits — for instance, if they fail to allocate allowances on time, or they give out unscheduled advances — it's unlikely that their children will view the new system as anything different than the way they've always done things. Parents must be every bit as diligent as their children, if not more so, if their children are to take the new system seriously and internalize the experiences and learning.

> Parents must be every bit as diligent as their children, if not more so, if their children are to take the new system seriously and internalize the experiences and learning.

How Kids
Learn About Money

Child psychologists say that children have the ability to take a symbol outside of themselves and let it represent them at the age of two. By the age of three, they begin to make abstract representative connections between objects and ideas. Author Neale S. Godfrey, former President of the First Women's Bank, founder of the First Children's Bank, and

Children pick up on the relationship between money and buying things at a very early age, as early as three years old.

Chairman of the Children's Financial Network, says that when your children understand that you go to the store and purchase items with money, they are ready to learn. Children pick up on the relationship between money and buying things at a very early age, as early as three years old. In a fortuitous coincidence, this is also the time when children are processing and internalizing an enormous amount of both observed and experiential data. For those of us who have children, it doesn't take scientific data and psychological testing to tell us that our children are master emulators of both the good and the bad in the world around them. Perhaps more than any other single psycho-social phenomenon, emulation is responsible for the steady march of progress toward the world as we know it now. We've all heard the phrases "monkey see, monkey do" and "if so-and-so jumped off a bridge, would you jump, too?" directed at children who have a tendency to follow the lead of their friends, generally into trouble. Perhaps there's a little more truth in those euphemisms than we'd like to admit.

The truth is that children are constantly internalizing relevant experiences and processing information as they develop their personality.

The truth is that children are constantly internalizing relevant experiences and processing information as they develop their personality.

Experiences at a young age are strong reinforcement for developing personalities and, as kids grow older, function as a foundation for more formalized educational processes. This is why it's so important to instill fundamental principles at an early age. As the spectrum of life experiences forms the boundaries in which kids exist and function, having a strong basic value system molds and processes life information into useful knowledge and, in the best of all worlds, wisdom.

Experiential approaches to child psychology issues have become a major focus of therapists and psychologists within the last decade. Particular attention is being given early experiential learning processes and how they effect future growth and development. Most of the emphasis of the work in this area has been focused on how abuse and neglect effect a child's personality, but a great deal can be gleaned from findings about how children process and learn from experiences in general. In fact, it may be that the same paradigm child psychologists use in determining abuse and neglect can be applied to discuss neglect and abuse as it relates to a child's financial education. For instance, if a young child suffers physical neglect — perhaps he didn't eat for a couple of days because his parents left him alone when they were away — that child is likely to neglect his own kids when he grows up if the problems produced by the neglect are not addressed in a therapeutic environment early on. The same principle applies to a young child who has learned money management skills by watching her parents' irresponsible spending habits. She is very likely to commit the same mistakes as an adult. In both instances the experiences are highly impressive upon the child's personality because of both the age at which they occur and are processed, and the intensity of the experience's reinforcement.

> The same paradigm child psychologists use in determining abuse and neglect can be applied to discuss neglect and abuse as it relates to a child's financial education.

Consequently, experiential learning has been used in a variety of situations that require a strong personal commitment and a solid foundation of principles in which new information is processed according to how it interfaces with previously learned commitments and values. The military uses experiential techniques extensively in training exercises and boot camp where live ammunition rounds are frequently used; the corporate marketplace applies it to internships and apprenticeships; politics makes use of experiential learning with its vast system of aids and assistants; and it can be used for something as ordinary as learning to ride a bike in which there's no other way to learn except through trial and error. And as in learning to ride a bike, once you learn it, it's learned forever because the experience is so profound that it imprints itself very strongly upon your personality.

It's precisely for these reasons that I advocate an experiential approach when teaching children about financial responsibility. As your child encounters new experiences and is forced to deal with them, strong connections are forged and decisions are reinforced, either negatively or positively, as kids either conquer or succumb to each new experience. When learning takes place in a structured system provided by the parents, children are able to develop a context and thus establish their own foundation for future learning. In other words, do it and the skills will come.

> In any educational situation, the parameters and structure within which learning takes place is frequently as important as the learning itself.

The structure that parents give to their children is extremely important. In any educational situation, the parameters and structure within which learning takes place is frequently as important as the learning itself. If you don't understand the rules for the game of basketball, it really doesn't matter if you know how to dribble a ball. If the point is to master the game, you need to know the rules in addition to the skills of dribbling, shooting, and passing.

Drawing upon my experiences both as a financial analyst and parent, I've devised a system whereby financial responsibility may be taught to children using a pragmatic, hands-on teaching technique that allows children to teach themselves through the experience of managing their own money. The Four-Part Money Management System involves teaching children how to responsibly spend, save, give and invest their money so that they may participate first-hand in the dynamics of financial responsibility.

It's no secret that corporate marketing departments have your kids' number when it comes to selling. That number was nearly $100 billion spent by kids in 1995. Eager to get their hands on as much of that as possible, companies spent a cool billion dollars — up from 100 million in 1980 — to sell things to your kids. The message marketing departments are sending to your children is that they are not lovable without whatever product they're trying to sell them.

Kids spent nearly $100 billion in 1995. Eager to get their hands on as much of that as possible, companies spent a cool billion dollars — up from 100 million in 1980 — to sell things to your kids.

The message marketing departments are sending to your children is that they are not lovable without whatever product the companies are trying to sell them.

By symbolizing and popularizing their products, marketing departments are playing upon your children's sense of self-worth and self-esteem. Quite simply, your children are not as good as they could be if they had the latest, greatest product which their company just happens to sell.

Recent surveys have shown that displaying anti-social behavior in commercials sells products. The survey focused on boys, but there are indications that the same philosophy works for girls. For proof, one has to look only as far as a recent soda pop commercial where teenage girls are vandalizing building facades with spray paint, and a perfume commercial where a young girl drives recklessly down a highway, stopping every so often to pick up a string of scraggly, dangerous-looking young men, and giving them a ride.

Kids' spending power is growing daily. Recent surveys show that 32% of high school students and 82% of college students have credit cards. The job of marketing departments and advertising firms, quite obviously and unashamedly, is to own young people and their $100 billion spending habit.

It doesn't take a psychologist to see that there is a war being waged for control of your child's attention and interest. Our children's generation will grapple with difficult social and financial issues like health care and tax reform. The prospect of a generation raised on the kind of financial responsibility that is being taught currently is almost frightening, especially since my kids will be deciding, for the most part, on how to take care of me in my old age. How will our children be able to participate responsibly in the political process? How will they be able to understand important financial issues like budgets and taxes and interest rates and health care reform and the like, and cast their vote in an informed, enlightened and responsible manner if they don't

Recent surveys show that 32% of high school students and 82% of college students have credit cards.

have at least a basic understanding of financial management?

How will they be able to understand
important financial issues like budgets
and taxes and interest rates and health
care reform and the like, and cast their
vote in an informed, enlightened and
responsible manner if they don't have at
least a basic understanding of financial
management?

The answer, quite clearly, is that they won't.
That is why I cannot stress strongly enough the
importance of getting your children started now on
the basics of financial responsibility and instilling in
them the kind of financial values that will serve them
and our society in the future. It's been said many
times, information is power. Add to that financial
management skills, and you empower your children
to change the world and create their own future.

Resources

Books

Alexander, Who Used To Be Rich Last Sunday, by Judith Viorst (Aladdin Books). A boy's money burns a hole in his pocket. (primary)

Part III

Applying
the
Money Management
System

Chapter 8

The Allowance System

The per capita income in the United States is huge compared with other nations, but how much you bring in is not really important. It doesn't make much difference what your tax bracket is because the same money management principles apply at every income level. What is important is what you do with the money you have. No matter how much you make, it can still all go away. And even if you have just a little, it is still possible to save and invest a small portion of it. If you pay yourself first, and save and invest even a very small percentage of your income over long periods of time, you will be financially successful.

The same money management principles that effect you also apply to your children. No matter what your family income bracket, it's important to teach your kids how to handle the money they do have, how to set realistic goals, and how to make it work for them so they can meet their goals and get what they want.

When money isn't managed in a consistent, disciplined fashion, it often causes friction in couples. And the money concerns that cause problems between parents also tend to crop up between parents and children. It's common in most households for kids and parents to bicker over money matters. Parents have money and kids want it, or want to buy something with it, and don't know any other way to get it than to whine and complain and beg and demand. You're familiar with the scratched record syndrome:

"Can I have my allowance?"

"I never have any money, Dad."

"Mom, will you buy me this."

"Well, you never give me that."

"Can I have $10 for the movies?"

Parents complain in return that their kids are making them go broke.

"When I was your age . . . ."

"I'm not made of money, you know."

"Money doesn't grow on trees."

There is a constant struggle over money between parents and their kids. Why? Because kids don't have their own source of income. If they're under the age of 16 or so, they're probably not working, and if they're under the age of 12, they legally aren't allowed to work. That means that kids under the age of 16 don't have access to a source of income. Mom and Dad are just flipping them money, usually on an ad hoc basis, and the kids are learning bad habits. Their self esteem gets no boost because the money they do get is just a gift or an afterthought. They have no motivation to spend or save it wisely. There are no rules around it. Your current allowance plan is probably limited to giving your kids money when they ask or when you think of it, and they run out and

> Mom and Dad are just flipping them money, usually on an ad hoc basis, and the kids are learning bad habits. Their self esteem gets no boost because the money they do get is just a gift or an afterthought.

spend it as it comes in. An allowance is a good starting point for teaching your kids about money management because it can be controlled and recorded.

"One of the biggest mistakes parents
make is not giving enough (allowance).
Kids need adequate funds if they're going
to practice making sound financial decisions."

— Bonnie Drew
(author of *MoneySkills:
101 Activities to Teach
Your Child About Money*)

More than
88% of those
surveyed
learned
everything
they knew
about money
from their
parents.

A survey of junior high and highschool students
commissioned by Liberty Financial in 1993 showed
that more than 88% of those surveyed learned everything they knew about money from their parents.
Kids need to have money, a source of income, so that
they can learn to handle money properly on their
own. My 12-year-old gets an allowance of $12 a
week, and that's a lot, especially if she just goes out
and blows it on junk. But with our allowance plan,
in which she doesn't get any money for another
week, and she spends, gives, saves, and invests it
properly, $12 is actually not very much. She has to
live pretty frugally to get by on that, to accomplish
all the things she wants to accomplish. Considering
their cost of living, seven-year-olds need a bare min-

imum of $1 a week and 10-year-olds at least $3 in order to do any serious spending and saving.

A lot of people look at our family allowance system and say, "Gosh, that's a lot of money." But we're teaching our kids to stand on their own two feet. They are learning by experience that money is in limited supply, that their allowance is all they get. It's a mistake not to give your kids an allowance.

In 1993, more than 49% of children ages six to 14 did not have a weekly allowance; 37% received an allowance on a regular basis; and 14% received money as needed. Of the kids who did not have an allowance, over 57% received less than $5 a week; 25% received between $5 and $10, and only 18% received more.

Why do kids need a regular and reliable source of income? They need a source of income to (a) Learn that money is in limited supply, and (b) To have something to learn with. You don't learn how to play baseball without a ball and bat, and you don't learn how to swim without going into the water. And you're not going to learn how to manage money without getting some in your hands. In order to learn how to handle money, kids need to have a source of income, which initially should be their allowance until they are old enough to have jobs.

Money management is like a row boat. Allowance is one oar and managing the allowance is the other oar. And if you pull on just one oar, you will just go in circles, but if you pull both of them together, you will make progress through life. It's important to provide your children with a source of income — that's the allowance — but second of all, and just as important, you need to teach them how to handle that money once they have it.

> They need a source of income to (a) Learn that money is in limited supply, and (b) To have something to learn with.

> "Surveys have shown that children who get no allowances receive roughly as much money from their parents as children who do, but those on a regular allowance learn more about managing money."
>
> — Linda Vanhoose

Another mistake is giving an advance on an allowance.

I hear from parents that they didn't get an allowance when they were kids so they're sure not giving their kids one. Or they give their kids an allowance and still supplement it during the week. One woman I know told me she gives her six-year-old daughter 25¢ a day every day.

I asked her, "So if it's Tuesday afternoon and you are at Wal-Mart and your daughter sees something she really wants and asks you for it, are you going to buy it for her?"

The mother replied that it depends on whether or not she has the money and whether she really feels in the mood to buy something. Since the mother is really not sticking to an allowance, the 25¢ is basically discretionary money because the daughter gets more during the week on a situational basis. When I asked how much money the mother was giving her daughter during the week, if she includes the things she buys for her, she hadn't any idea; no clue. That's a mistake; parents are treating money lightly so their kids treat it lightly. The biggest mistake is no allowance at all. The second is not sticking to the allowance.

Another common mistake is not helping kids manage their allowance and their other sources of income such as when Grandma or Grandpa give them $10 for the holiday. What kids do with their money is important — how they manage it.

Another mistake is giving an advance on an allowance. It usually happens spontaneously, when you're at the store and your child wants something he sees and says he will repay you out of his piggy bank when you get home. You loan him $5, he forgets, you never see it again and you also forget or don't ask him for it. You have now taught your child the concept of debt. He's learned that it's okay to treat debt lightly. You are not showing him the basic principles of sound debt management. That is why debt is to be avoided.

Money management is important because, psychologically and emotionally and physically, we all have to have money to survive and function in this world. Since that's a given, why not create a system that's simple and straightforward and that removes the stress of money between parents and children?

The Allowance System

The Four-Part Money Management System for kids consists of spending, giving, saving, investing. The allowance you give your kids is the financing for the method, the foundation. Without that allowance, all the money management systems in the world are useless because there's nothing tangible for your kids to practice on. Without an allowance, all you've got is a theory of money management.

The allowance system is simplicity itself.

> The allowance you give your kids is the financing for the method, the foundation.

It's Saturday morning and you say to your children, "Here's your allowance and you don't get any more until next Saturday."

That's it. You're done. It's up to them to make it last until next Saturday. They have to save a portion, spend a portion, give a portion, and invest a portion, but once you've taught them how to do that, it's their responsibility, not yours.

If you and your kids agree upon a few simple rules about allowance, everyone will be a whole lot happier in the long run.

For starters, pick a regular time when allowance will be paid. This will eliminate a lot of potential begging, whining, and hand tugging. Now, I'm not suggesting that it be as specific as Tuesday at 2:17 p.m., but agree on a general time, like Saturday morning, and stick to it.

In general, at least for kids who are just starting out, getting paid an allowance once a week is much easier for them to manage than getting paid only once a month. A lot of families find that weekends are a little less hectic and easier to schedule than during the week (unless you're in my family when Saturdays mean three separate soccer games, lessons, friends' birthday parties, and concerts, and that's just before noon).

You just have to be vigilant so that when you go to the store and your kids say, "Mom, get me this, Dad, get me that," you remind them that they get their allowance on Saturday. Period. No more. Otherwise you violate the entire system. You don't give them any advances on their allowance, either. An advance on an allowance is a form of debt and a bad habit to initiate, even if it's only for three days. Remember, the whole idea of getting an allowance is for kids to learn how to manage their money. At some point they're going to run out of allowance money. I guarantee it. Stand firm, no matter how much they drop their lower lips and complain. If you cave in, your kids aren't learning anything except how to manipulate you.

You need to teach your kids about money. How you teach your kids about money is to teach them to spend it right, save it, give it, invest it. The place to start right now, today, is set your kids up with an allowance system. According to a recent Nickelodeon/Yankelovich Youth Monitor U.S. survey, six to eight-year-olds receive $1.99 to $3.80 a week in allowance; nine to 11-year-olds, $4.17 to $4.80; and 12 and 13-year-olds, $5.82.

How much should you give your child? I suggest that $1 for every year of age is a proper allowance to give your child every week. A six-year-old gets $6, a 12-year-old gets $12, a 17-year-old gets $17. Even your two-year-old gets $2. That's not too young to start even though it will be several years until they can understand some of the finer points of money management. It's good to introduce a regular allowance at least by age six.

"Allowance is the best tool for teaching kids to be smart money managers. It gives them first-hand experience budgeting, saving and making spending decisions."

— Ray Guarendi
(child psychologist, quoted in a 1995 issue of *Working Mother* magazine)

According to a recent Nickelodeon/ Yankelovich Youth Monitor U.S. survey, six to eight-year-olds receive $1.99 to $3.80 a week in allowance; nine to 11-year-olds, $4.17 to $4.80; and 12 and 13-year-olds, $5.82.

As part of the allowance system, I suggest you cut your children off at age 18. By 18, if they've been managing their allowance for a number of years, they should be ready to earn and manage their own money unless you want to fund them through college. That is totally up to the parents. Once they're between 12 and 15, your kids are ready to start babysitting or mowing lawns or find some other way to earn extra income because $16 a week allowance is not enough for 16-year-olds to do the things they want to do. They want Nikes or team jackets or a fancy hairdryer, things that are very expensive, so they need to earn the additional money they'll need to pay for these extras.

Getting Started

All right, Jason or Jessica, we're starting over. Beginning today. I just finished this book and it said to do it and it sounds like a good idea. It's not my fault, it's the book's fault. So here it is, a clean break. We're starting from scratch. Here's what we're going to do; every Saturday morning by 10 a.m. you are going to have your allowance. You're going to get a dollar for every year of age. What I want you to do the minute you get that money is to run up to your bedroom and divide it into thirds: One third you can spend any way you like, one third you save, and one third you can invest. Don't worry about what those are now, we'll get to that later. You have to make that one third that is spending money last because I am not going to give you any more money during the week. No advances, no candy when we're at the store, nada. Come next Saturday morning, you've got your allowance again. Those are the rules. Now, for Christmas you are going to get nice things and on your birthday, you're going to get stuff. Grandma might send you presents, but when Grandma sends you money, you do the same thing with it: Run to your bedroom and divide it into thirds. We're starting all over. From now on, you can have anything you want to have. You see a doll in the store, a bicycle, candy, if you want it, you can have it. Anything.

The kids are going, "Yeah!" But remember the rules. They buy whatever it is with their money, not with yours.

You know you need to teach your kids about drugs or they are going to learn it on their own, and what they learn can lead to a bad habit. It's the same with money. If you don't teach your kids yourself, nobody else is going to do it for you. Schools won't teach them, they're not going to find it on the Internet or on a CD-ROM, they're not going to hear it at their church or synagogue or mosque. You can let them figure it out for themselves, probably wrongly, or you can teach them.

The Benefits
of the Allowance System

If you teach your children how to handle money properly, they learn the value of discipline and ground rules. Kids want to know the rules. They need to know the rules. Even a football game would-n't be any fun if there were no rules and no referees. You need to have basic discipline and that alone — the discipline of handling money properly — will actually relieve a lot of stress from the situation.

When you teach your children money management principles, it takes the heat off, it takes the pressure off, and the parents don't have to be the bad guys any more. You don't have to continually turn down your kids when they ask for things.

"No, you can't buy that, it's too expensive."

If you are consistent about the new allowance plan, your kids will learn quickly that it does no good to ask for things. Now, all of a sudden, it becomes their problem, the children's problem. And that's how they learn.

They also learn how to handle delayed gratification because they are saving and investing some of their allowance for the future. My daughter decided to do the pie thing; she sold $350 worth of pies so she could go skiing. My wife cried when we put her on the bus on a Saturday morning. There was a bus load of about 40 kids and I'll guarantee you my daughter was the only one who paid her own way. She paid for everything, her ski rental, her lessons, her bus ride, and there was so much pride in that little girl when she got on that bus. This is the same little girl who, a year ago, would have just hit up Mom and Dad for the trip.

It was really hard for me when I saw how hard she was working to pay for that trip. She must have baked 50 pies, homemade pies. It took her three days. I wanted to buy the ingredients for her, but I didn't. It almost seemed cruel, but now that it's done, she is so much better and happier for it.

She enjoyed everything about that ski trip, even the bus ride, everything, even though she didn't know anyone else on the bus. She was supposed to go with a friend of hers but when it turned cold, the friend canceled out. But my daughter said that was okay with her; she said she was not going to wait for her friends to make her happy.

"I'm going. I worked hard for it, and I'm going."

And she had a great time. The other kids were complaining about how tired they were — their parents paid for the trip and they could afford an attitude. Not her, she was living it up.

Being in charge of their own money feeds into children's sense of self-esteem and their place in the community. In the larger picture, earning money is important beyond just the choices it offers.

> Being in charge of their own money feeds into children's sense of self-esteem and their place in the community.

Chores

Once kids understand how to handle their allowance properly, then they are naturally going to want to get more money. They start thinking about all the things they could do if they really put their mind to it. They want to go to the next step which is going out and earning more money on their own — getting their own money to manage.

The next question, naturally, is what about chores? Do you pay your kids to do the chores? Do you hinge the allowance on the successful completion of chores? Most experts agree that there are two different lessons to be learned, one from allowance and a different one from chores, and that neither lesson is learned when the two are inter-connected. An allowance should be an innate benefit of belonging to the family. Allowance is a right, not payment for good behavior or for work, nor is it a privilege. It provides the money with which your children will learn about money management and prioritizing and shopping for value and spending wisely. Assigning chores, on the other hand, teaches children about community responsibility and good citizenship.

> An allowance should be an innate benefit of belonging to the family.

Human beings naturally congregate in groups who share some common bond. In a family, the group bond is kinship. In a church or synagogue, the

Chores, on the other hand, teach children about community responsibility and good citizenship.

members are bound by their religious beliefs. In a town or city, the residents share services they all need such as water and street maintenance and police protection. In any community, everyone needs to participate, to do their share, for both the individual and the common good. Adults aren't paid to take out their trash for the garbage truck; they aren't paid to vote; they aren't paid to shovel snow off the sidewalks in front of their houses in the winter. These adult chores are necessary to the well being of the community and all pitch in voluntarily.

Children learn about the importance of community responsibility by doing chores at home: washing the dishes, taking out the trash, helping to cook dinner. The entire household benefits from the chores being done. When each family member has chores assigned, it provides a sense of togetherness. So no, you don't pay your kids to do chores. You establish a set of chores for the kids to do that they are responsible for, but you don't pay them. If you do, they'll hold you ransom and they won't do anything else without getting paid for it.

Parents should sit down with their children and decide which chores each family member will do and on what schedule. A weekly chore list, posted on the refrigerator, makes assigned chores easier to remember. Put Mom and Dad's name on the chore list as well. It demonstrates to the kids that they're not being asked to do more than their share and reminds them that the whole family is working together. Let the kids mark completed chores with a star or sticker to give them a sense of accomplishment.

You can't expect your kids to accomplish chores as efficiently or as thoroughly as an adult would. Try doing a chore with them the first few times until they get the hang of it. And let them be creative about how to accomplish the chore. They don't have to do it exactly the same way you do. By letting them experiment you show that you value their input.

When you tie allowance payment to the successful completion of chores, you run into a number of problems. There may be a difference in how an adult and a child define "successfully completed." Does the child have to meet adult standards? What if the job is only partially completed? Kids resent parents who hold them ransom. I remember an occasion when I was young when I sat at the dinner table staring down a plate of cold brussel sprouts for an hour after the rest of the family had finished eating. I was not allowed to leave the table until I cleaned my plate. It's the same type of "being held for ransom" and didn't accomplish what my parents intended. To this day I resent them for it and I still can't eat a brussel sprout.

It accomplishes nothing except a parental demonstration of power to tie allowance and chores to a reward/punishment cycle. Allowance is a family privilege and chores are a civic responsibility. Help your kids learn by keeping the two lessons separate.

Resources

Books

It's My Money, by Ann Banks (Puffin, 1993).

Videos

"Enhancing the Financial Literacy of Older Youth" 1994 Teleconference; 2 hour videotape, available from the University of Idaho for $29.95.

Internet

Judith Briles: *Raising Money-Wise Kids*
http://www.briles.com/books/book_moneykids.html

Chapter 9

How To Make Money Make Sense To Children

Your kids observe your spending and saving habits and they're likely to imitate you. If you and your spouse deal directly with finances, discuss differences calmly, and find positive solutions, your children will be far more likely to learn how to handle money rationally. The topic of money is often emotionally loaded and can also mean power — control of one person over another. To help separate money from these emotions, include your children in a family money discussion on topics you feel confident will stay under control, like how much to spend on Christmas gifts or spring vacation or a new computer.

What motivates kids to deposit their dollars, dimes and sometimes pennies week after week? The same thing that motivates adults: a sense of control. Kids take financial direction primarily from their parents until approximately age ten. After that, peers become the major influence. Kids who learn about money early are often pretty good at making it later.

Teaching children about finances isn't a one-time event, but a process that continues throughout childhood — and the sooner you begin, the better. Between six and 11 are prime ages for establishing a full slate of financial skills.

Our church was planning a new sanctuary but one Sunday morning our pastor announced that there was a delay in the building program. The construction crew that was going to lay the foundation had cleared away an auto dealership to make space to put up our building. Under the auto dealership they found a big tank that was used for fuel dumping, probably as big as two large rooms, buried directly beneath where they were going to put the foundation. There were two options: They could either pull the tank out, and six feet of soil around it, refill the hole with dirt, and then lay the foundation and build the building, or they could just skip all that and build the building. The problem was that the tank and earth around it couldn't support the infrastructure for the new building. If they had tried to build the sanctuary over the tank it would have caved in. You've got to start over — go in and gut the shaky foundation before you can lay a solid new one.

Teaching kids about money is similar. You've got to rip away the bad foundation and lay a new one before you start a financial infrastructure or the system is going to cave in some day. Complicated financial systems and online banking and debit cards and whatnot are the infrastructure that our kids have to live with. If you don't give them a firm foundation, that infrastructure could cave in on them. If you help them construct a foundation now, the coming financial transaction technology will make life easier for them instead of more complicated.

Regardless of the technology, the basic principles of money management stay the same even though ten years from now the look might be totally

What motivates kids to deposit their dollars, dimes and sometimes pennies week after week? The same thing that motivates adults: a sense of control.

You've got to rip away the bad foundation and lay a new one before you start a financial infrastructure or the system is going to cave in some day.

different. Technology that's right over the horizon is leading toward transactions without anything you can touch. That's the real world our kids are going to be living in so prepare them now before things get more complicated. A viable money system foundation has staying power.

Equip your kids with a good sound philosophy of money because that will never change. It's not complicated — it's always been the same essentially — it's just the look that changes. The philosophy is timeless: spend, give, save and invest. Even though the currencies and the materials we use can and do change, the principles won't. If you instill principles now, your children will be able to apply them no matter what currency they use and no matter what online banking system they have.

Many parents ask me why they should teach their kids about money. Why not wait until they're older. Well, guess what? You're teaching them whether you want to or not. They are watching what you do; they're watching how you act. No matter what you do, they are learning from you now, so why not teach them the right principles. If you don't do it, nobody else is going to.

"Never spend your money before you have it."

— Thomas Jefferson

If kids have money and know how to manage it, there wont' be any stress from money in their lives;

they'll be free to focus on other things that are more constructive: free to travel, free to accomplish and, if nothing else, free to give the money away. If they want to build a business, they can go do that. When money creates choices, it is a positive. The goal is financial independence. That doesn't necessarily mean rich, but it does mean in control. Your kids will have money to survive and operate in this world so teach them a system that's simple and straightforward and that will take the stress out of money.

Teaching a money management system is analogous to teaching your kids good health and nutrition habits. Health and nutrition today appear very complicated even though the principles are simple. Good health habits are not a trendy phase or a cycle. They are a simple lifetime habit of eating a good balanced diet and getting exercise. So many people are looking for the next quick fix and the idea of an unchanging, basic philosophy has almost lost all meaning. Money is the same thing. People make it complicated when it's not. There are so many choices that it's easy to get lost in the shuffle. With a good sound solid foundation — the Four-Part Money Management System — your kids will be able to intelligently sort through the morass of options. They won't be constantly dependent on someone else's advice or expertise.

One woman I know made tons of money running a very successful business. She didn't know anything about money management and couldn't be bothered to learn so she turned it all over to her accountant and he ran off with it to Mexico.

> So many people are looking for the next quick fix and the idea of an unchanging, basic philosophy has almost lost all meaning.

Why A Four-Part System?

By now you probably are aware that there are lots of books and products aimed at teaching your kids about money, and many of them offer useful information. But they are all piecemeal — none of them offer a comprehensive, all inclusive system and underlying philosophy. There's one product that helps teach kids how to use a checkbook. Another, Christian-oriented product is a piggy bank in the shape of a church. There are books that explain the stock market. But there is not one that introduces the concept of long-term investing or its importance. Some discuss how to start a business or earn extra money. There's not one that covers the four essential and inter-related issues of a sound approach to money management — spending, giving, saving and investing.

The Four-Part Money Management System could be a six-part system by including allowance and earning money, or a seven-part system by adding how to start a business. But the basis of the Four-Part System is what you do with the money you have, regardless of how you get it, whether it's allowance, earned, a gift, or winning the lottery. About the only other possibilities beyond spending, giving, saving and investing money are throwing it away — an extreme form of spending — or stashing it under your mattress, which is just an ineffective method of saving. The bottom line is you either get rid of the money you have by spending it or giving it away, or you keep the money you have by saving and investing it.

Why all four at once? Because life is unpredictable. None of us can plan for all contingencies, whether good or bad, but you need to be able to take advantage of them or handle them when they arise.

There is always going to be something we want that costs more than our weekly cash flow — a vacation, a car, a trip: savings. We need to be able to pay for the big tag items when they occur in our lives — college, a wedding, babies, retirement: investing. We need to be able to pay for our regular survival needs — groceries, gas, clothing: spending. And we need to participate responsibly in our community, our world: giving. They are all equally important in the way they impact our lives and all four need to be attended to at the same time.

The Money Management System described throughout this book is different than every other money management system because this is the only one that adequately addresses investing. And that is probably the most important thing that kids can learn. You can teach kids how to spend money properly but if they do that, they will probably spend everything they have and they will always be broke just like most Americans who today have a very low savings rate.

The savings rate in this country is only three to four percent while every other developed nation has nearly twice that rate. The low rate here is not due to lack of opportunity, and it's not because of a lack of knowledge, but because we don't train our children how to handle money properly. This System teaches kids once and for all to pay themselves first with a portion of their money that is invested and not spent. That's true savings; that's true long-term investment into their future and not just money that they park temporarily until they spend it. Other systems out there pretty much advocate a system where kids spend some money, give some money, and then put some money away for savings, which is eventually spent. So basically the kids are always broke.

The Rules — Getting Started

Now it's time to learn a simple system that works so you can hit the ground running. Now that you have all the philosophy in your mind and you have all the reasoning for teaching your kids about money, here's what you do. This section is about how to apply everything that has been discussed.

Changing the ground rules and establishing a new routine, until it becomes habit, can be difficult. Parents and kids all have so many automatic responses to situations, so both parents and kids need to learn new habits. The key is to apply the philosophy as simply as possible. The kids are going to be rooted in their old habits and likely to be whining or expecting the old interaction about money so, for a while during the transition period, it's going to seem a lot easier for you to just give in. But don't.

What you do is walk into your kid's life and just totally turn it upside down. That's the best way to apply this program. You don't phase it in over time; you don't gradually adapt to it. You just totally change. You explain the new rules and then stick to them, no matter what! You can't weasel around or make exceptions or give in once in a while. It has to be done in a clear, clean break. Without question, if the Four-Part Money Management System fails, it fails because of the parents, not because of the kids. I hear parents all the time say "Oh, this works great. It's incredible. It does everything promised."

Then I hear other parents say, "Well, it didn't really work for us." When I ask why, they answer they don't know, they just didn't really use it that much.

The rules are simple. You give your kids their allowance, the same amount at the same time each week. The kids immediately divide their money: one

> What you do is walk into your kid's life and just totally turn it upside down.

third for spending and giving, one third for saving, and one third for investing (the next four chapters explain each of these areas). The easiest way to do that is to have three labeled containers, mason jars work well, to physically separate the money being allocated for each area.

Do the containers for the money have to be locked? It's helpful if they are; they don't need a padlock but at least physically show the kids that the money shouldn't go anywhere. Even a temporary lock is okay, but the money definitely should be locked up. A locking bank is absolutely recommended for the investment money, if nothing else. The lock helps children keep the image in their minds that the money is not to be touched. It's not important that its locked up like a safe which has a key. All it needs to be is an honor system. The lock is there more as a reminder to your children not to touch that money. It's not a padlock, and you don't have to police it. It's just simply a deterrent, a reminder to keep the kids in stride with the system and keep them focused on what they're doing.

How do parents prevent kids from raiding their giving, saving, and investing funds for spending money? The best way to do that is to really teach the kids the disciplines of the thirds, to separate the money physically. Tell the kids it's the rule, "You must separate your money, and if you violate that then you may also violate your privilege of getting an allowance." I don't suggest disciplining kids with money; however, I do suggest if you're giving your children an allowance and they don't manage that money properly, then you shouldn't give them the allowance until they learn how to handle it. Parents have to really work closely with the children on this. You need to sit down with your children and explain to them that this is an allowance that they are given and the only reason they will continue to get it is if

"Here are the rules: A third of it is for spending and giving; a third of is for saving; and a third is for investing."

you know that they are learning from it and handling the money correctly. You've got to do this or you're not going to get an allowance anymore.

"Here are the rules: A third of it is for spending and giving; a third is for saving; and a third is for investing. The third that goes into investing never gets spent, it only gets invested. The third that is in savings and the third that is in spending eventually all get spent but for different types of things."

That's it. The same rules apply for any other money they get. It's up to you, the parents, not to give them any money other than their allowance. You can treat them to a movie or take them out for ice cream, but don't give them money on demand. When Grandma sends them $20 for a present, they treat it the same way, dividing it in thirds. They treat it the same way whether it's from Grandma, from mowing the law, or from an allowance. They should follow the Four-Part Money Management System regardless of how the money comes into their hands. Grandma will probably give them more money when she knows they will handle it correctly.

How do you get the System started? You sit down with your kids and say, "All right, kids, here are the new rules. You can have whatever you want with no interference from me, but you have to pay for it. If what you want is expensive, you will have to save for it. You know how you are always bugging me for gum or candy or soda at the store? You can buy that now but it has to come out of your spending allowance. I am not going to say no, but I'm not going to pay for it. You are. At church, you will put your own money into the plate and if you want to do something to save the rain forests or help the homeless or to support some other good cause, you will use the money in your giving account. You will invest 30% of your money for the future. You won't touch it otherwise.

Explain the System, show them how to allocate their money, help them devise a physical way to separate their money, and then stick to it. Put the rules on a recipe card and stick it in your wallet with your money to remind yourself if you have to, but don't break the plan.

It's the parents who have to be prepared because the parents set the rules. It's like the coach telling the new football players, "All right you guys, there's a curfew now. You have to be in by midnight before a football game." There can be no exceptions and no second chances. The kid coming in at 1 a.m. doesn't play the next day, period. You have to stick with the new rules no matter what or you'll create bigger problems than there were before.

> It's the parents who have to be prepared because the parents set the rules.

What happens when you slip up? Admit it to your child immediately. If you forget and buy your child a pack of gum at the store, as soon as you remember, tell your child, "That was my mistake. I forgot the rules," and then go back to the program immediately.

What if your kids slip up. Let them. They're going to anyway. They'll make mistakes, blunders, flubs, and glaring errors, not once but many times. But still let them. The best way for them to learn from this System is by their own experience, not yours. Have faith. They'll get it right eventually.

Benefits of the System

The Four-Part Money Management System offers some fringe benefits in addition to giving kids a fiscal education. Money is inextricably woven into the fabric of life. If you teach your kids how to handle money properly, they will indirectly benefit in other

Money is
inextricably
woven into
the fabric of
life.

ways that will help them build a life-long value system. They will practice life skills that they will need to live successfully no matter what they do and no matter how much or how little money they make as adults.

Self-Reliance. Because being responsible for their own money is simple, fun and rewarding, it motivates kids to do things on their own rather than just go to Mom and Dad to get it. It allows them to have choices about what to do with their time and their money. They can make the decision about where to invest and what to spend their money on without interference.

It allows
them to have
choices
about what
to do with
their time
and their
money.

Discipline. It provides discipline and some ground rules. Kids want to know the rules. They need to know the rules. What fun would a soccer game be if there were no rules and no referees? The basic discipline of handling money properly will actually relieve a lot of stress in the situation.

Prioritizing. With only so much available to spend, they have to decide what they really want to spend it on, which is another way of saying they need to establish their priorities. Parents don't need to say a word. If your kids blow their money on candy and the video arcade and then don't have enough at the end of the week to buy the new Hootie and the Blowfish CD they can't live without, or maybe Chutes and Ladders for younger kids, they're going to figure out prioritizing on their own pretty fast. In just a few weeks they're going to sit down and decide what's really important to them and what isn't.

Goal Setting. If there is something they want they can't afford, they soon realize they need to save up for three weeks to get it or need to go shovel snow off driveways. They have to devise a plan and then go out and apply it. It takes the pressure off the parents. The parents don't have to always be opening their wallet every time they turn around.

Planning Ahead. Once your child has identified and defined a goal, he has to figure out how to achieve that goal. One of the benefits of money management is that it makes kids think and plan ahead. Goals that require more money than is immediately available mean thinking long term and developing a budget; how much of the weekly spending money needs to be set aside for how many weeks to achieve the goal.

Delayed Gratification. All adults know that it is close to impossible to instantly indulge their wants and needs. Despite the increased speed at which the world works with e-mail and faxes and overnight package delivery, Christmas still doesn't come in April, you can't stop the rain because you have a picnic planned, and even on the Concord, you can't get to the other side of the country in a few minutes. For most things we want we need to identify the goal, plan ahead, and then wait. When parents indulge their children by giving them whatever they want the moment they want it, they're doing them a disservice. The kids are going to be sorely disappointed when they get older and find out that instant gratification is not the way it really works. Both the saving and investing portions of the plan show kids the value of delayed gratification.

If you could give only one piece of advice
to parents about raising financially
responsible kids, what would it be?
"Instill the concept of saving for
something in them. Steer kids away
from instant gratification."

— Cynthia Oti
(investment expert)

Mistakes Are Part
of the Process

Mistakes with money are going to happen. Count on it. Parents make mistakes with money and your kids will, too.

A child should recognize a mistake and you should help him or her learn from it. But resist the temptation to get angry, judgmental, or hurt when your kid goofs. It's easier to learn and remember when there's an occasional mistake than from events that unfold without a hitch. The more constructively involved you are, the less likely it will be that your child will make a serious blunder. As in other areas of life, if your children feel you are open, they will seek your advice and appreciate your help.

Resources

Books

Making Cents: Every Kid's Guide To Money, by Elizabeth Wilkinson (Little Brown, 1989).

Money Doesn't Grow On Trees: A Parents' Guide to Raising Financially Responsible Children, by Neale S. Godfrey (Simon & Schuster, 1994; $11).

Internet

Family Education Network
http://www.familyeducation.com

Kids & Money
http://ndsuext.nodak.edu/extnews/pipeline/d-parent.htm

Kiplinger's Money-Smart Kids
http://www.kiplinger.com/store/kids.html

Teaching Kids Money Sense
http://www.kron.com/nc4/contact4/stories/kid-money.html

World of Money
http://www.worldofmoney.com

Chapter 10

The Value Of A Dollar Spent

Learning how to manage spending money is the first part of the Four-Part Money Management System. One third of your children's allowance money is allotted to spending and giving. Children and their parents usually consider spending to be the fun part. Your kids are allowed to do anything they want with this portion. They're in charge, no questions asked. But it means they can't whine and complain and beg and cajole you to buy them things anymore. They're on their own, and no advances on allowance either. When they run out during the week, before their next allowance is due — and they will run out — that's it. Spending experience, meaning trial and error, is the fastest teacher. For the first few weeks, or even months, your kids might blow their entire allowance on the day they receive it. They might spend all of it on what you consider junk: chewing gum, toys that break, the video arcade, fast food. If they're slow getting the point that they are not getting as much out of their money as they might, you can help them with a little comparative thinking. Ask them to consider how much pleasure they really got from the candy bar or fast food or video game for the money they spent on it as opposed to something they could enjoy more than once or for a longer time. Kids behavior changes pretty quickly once they're put in charge of their own money and not spending yours.

When I started using the System in my household, one of the first things I noticed that changed was when I took my kids to the movies. I might treat them to the price of a ticket, but they had to pay for their own snacks at the concession stand. It wasn't long before they were asking to bring treats from home instead of shelling out their own money for popcorn and cokes.

Kids 4-12 receive approximately $17 billion in total annual income and influence the spending of another $150 billion a year, yet have little instruction on how to manage money. They influence the purchase of everything from cold cereals to movies to fast food to vacation destinations. Almost all of kids' income is discretionary; only 5% is considered non-discretionary.

The earliest intuition kids have about money is about the power of spending it. They see parents enthusiasm for a coveted purchase or envying a new car model or thrilled with a new dress. "I need," is one of the most frequent phrases out of a kid's mouth. Learning the difference between needs and wants is the basis for almost all responsible money management. Needs are necessities: food, clothing, shelter, health. Wants make you feel comfortable or happy: jewelry, games, a haircut, new furniture. The difference between whether an item is a need or a want often depends on the situation. Do you want to read the book or is it required reading for a course you're taking? Does the new suit flatter your figure or do you need it for job interviews? Do you need a new computer for work you do at home or do you just want to cruise the Internet? Do you need an electric drill to rewire your house, or do you just want it to fill out your tool kit?

It's easy to send your kids mixed messages about needs and wants. Listen to yourself when you tell your child he doesn't need a new game, but you need to have your nails done professionally. Everyone's needs and wants are different depending on age, gender, climate, health, location, etc. A motorized mower may be a desired toy for a small lot in town, but a necessity on a farm. Most of a child's true needs are provided by their parents. Their spending money is discretionary, used for fulfilling wants.

Learning to differentiate between needs and wants is not a moral lesson but a lesson in reality. It's about available resources and cash flow, not right and wrong. Allow your kids some time to overcome their automatic "I want it now" impulse. To adjust, they have to internalize the difference between wanting and needing, and learn by experience that delayed gratification is still gratifying. Don't expect too much. It takes years of practice to differentiate

Learning the difference between needs and wants is the basis for almost all responsible money management.

Learning to differentiate between needs and wants is not a moral lesson but a lesson in reality.

between needs and wants and for them to learn to make spending decisions that are sensible for them. They're going to goof often. Let them. Kids will learn from their own experiences without their parents stuffing the lessons down their throat.

One way to help your kids understand the concept of value and how to make spending decisions is to suggest they make up the difference in price on large ticket items. For example, if your child needs new sneakers and wants the name brand $100 pair, but you feel the $50 pair is adequate, tell the child, "You need sneakers and I can afford to buy you the $50 pair. If you want the $100 pair, fine, but you pay the difference out of your spending money or savings." Children can usually see the logic and fairness in this kind of offer and, when it comes down to actually shelling out their own $50, reexamine their decision. If they have to pay the difference, which requires their giving up $50 of other, more alluring things they could do with that money, the $100 pair of sneakers probably won't seem quite so important. If they do decide that it's worth it and pay the extra $50, you can bet they're going to take very good care of those sneakers.

"Our kids learn consumer behaviors through watching what adults do. So it's really incumbent upon parents to try to get them to buy smartly. Start the learning process early, when the child is receptive to the message."

— Los Morton

(Cornell University)

When teaching your children about spending, start with the basics. It's easier to work out discretionary spending before taking on the necessities. Teach your kids how to walk before you teach them how to run. That means start by teaching them how to handle their allowance money. Parents should pay for their children's food, shelter, and clothing until their children are old enough to understand and truly grasp all the financial concepts. It might take a couple of years before your kids are ready to start managing their own clothing and food budgets, usually around age 14 or 15. The point here is to make sure your kids have a real good grasp of spending, giving, saving, and investing before starting them on food and clothing budgets. When they become responsible for some of their own necessities, you will probably have to give them a raise in allowance in order to cover those expenditures, but it's definitely advisable to initiate them at about age fourteen.

The point here is to make sure your kids have a real good grasp of spending, giving, saving, and investing before starting them on food and clothing budgets.

Older teens have more expenses than younger children and need to learn more financial self-reliance as they'll be on their own soon. Teens' income usually consists of allowance, job or business, and monetary gifts. Their expenses include: savings (one third of their income), investments (another third of their income), charitable donations, food (snacks, school lunches), entertainment (movies, video games, sports, CDs, dating), transportation (public, bicycle, or car), school supplies, clothing, clubs or hobbies, and a college fund. It's between parents and their teens to decide which items the teens are responsible for. Some parents have their teens pay for their own non-essential clothing and accessories, like paying the difference for a designer label. Whatever the decision in your home, make sure the list is specific and clearly defined.

"Because we live in an increasingly complicated world, it is more important than
ever to teach children to make intelligent
decisions regarding shopping, saving and
credit."

— Linda Vanhoose
(Knight-Ridder
Newspapers)

One way to help your teens to responsibly take
over paying for more of their own expenses is to suggest they make an estimate of their weekly expenses
and compare it with their income. If expenses
exceed income, suggest ways they can pare down
their expenses or consider an adjustment in
allowance.

A lot of the items teens will be paying for are
new expenses for them. To learn what things really
cost, they can get a small pocket notebook and use it
to write down the amount they spend for everything
they buy for one month. One page of the notebook
can be assigned to each category of expense like
food, toiletries, clothes, entertainment, etc. If they
want to try allotting a certain amount of their spending money for specific types of expenses, they can
write in the allotted amount at the top of the page and
deduct the amount they spend in that category, each
time they make a purchase, from the original
amount. That way, they'll always know how much
of their money is available for spending in that category.

The notebook also provides a tool for kids who want to figure out in advance how much something they want to do will cost them and whether they can afford it. If your child wants to spend a day at the amusement park, she can make a list of all things she will need to pay for to do it: transportation, entry ticket, food, rides, souvenirs. Once the list is complete, assign a dollar amount for each item on it. Compare the total against the available money and adjust the categories as necessary.

Anytime between ages two and 11 is a good time to start consumer training. By age three, about 66% of kids are already making verbal requests for products, and before age five, 75% of kids are picking items off the shelf.

Smart Shopping

Managing their own money isn't going to stop kids, or anyone else, from spending. But it will motivate them to learn more about how to shop wisely and become knowledgeable consumers. You can help them with this. Show them how to shop comparatively, how to find bargains, the advantage of waiting for a sale, calling ahead for the price before going to the store, and even clipping coupons and bulk buying. Go with them to the mall and compare the prices in upscale boutiques with the prices in department stores, and even in catalogs, for the same item.

Never ask of money spent
Where the spender thinks it went.
Nobody was ever meant
To remember or invent
What he did with every cent.

— Robert Frost

You can help your younger children pick up the concept of comparative shopping by taking them to the supermarket. While younger kids can't do the math, they can understand comparisons, small versus large cans, fresh versus old produce. Point out the difference in price between different brands of the same product. Anytime between ages two and 11 is a good time to start consumer training. By age three, about 66% of kids are already making verbal requests for products, and before age five, 75% of kids are picking items off the shelf.

Pre-schoolers get a lot of their consumer "education" from television. If you ever watch Saturday morning cartoons with your child, you'll probably hear, "Can I have that?" after almost every ad. The advertisers aren't dumb, they know how to make their product look bigger than life and more exciting than anything in the real world. And they seldom provide the information you really need to make a decision about whether the product is for you. As soon as your pre-schoolers can say, "Gimmie," they're old enough to start learning a little about the world of advertising. Kids are exposed to an average of 400 TV commercials a week, every one of them carrying the message, "buy this." The ads appeal to kids' sense of security, self-image, popularity, and status among peers. Take them to the store after a morning of TV ads aimed at kids, and let them compare the actual products with the image they have from the commercials. They'll figure out pretty quickly that the commercials make things look more glamorous than they really are, and that claims that the doll or kit is "only" $39.95 doesn't include the necessary batteries and accessories that were shown in the ad. Pretty soon you'll hear your kids responding to ads with healthy skepticism and feeling pretty darn proud of themselves for seeing through the ruse.

> Kids are exposed to an average of 400 TV commercials a week, every one of them carrying the message, "buy this."

Children in the 4 to 12 age group spend
$7.29 to $11 billion a year. Teens
spend $100 billion a year. Half of that
derives from allowance, a third from paid
work or chores, and the balance from
gifts of money.

Five year olds spend an average of
$2.81 a week, nine to 11-year-olds,
$4.80 a week, children 12 to 14, nearly
$28, and at 15 to 17, $43 a week.

Kids spend heavily in six areas: food, play items, clothing, movies, pre-recorded videos, video arcades, and other. Two billion dollars on junk food, 1.9 billion for toys and games, $800 million on movies, videos, shows, concerts, and sports events, $700 million on clothing, $486 million on arcade video games, $264 million on miscellaneous items from stereos to compact discs to cosmetics and jewelry and telephones and other living expenses, and $6 billion in savings.

Conventional wisdom cautions that you should never go shopping for groceries when you're hungry.

Conventional wisdom cautions that you should never go shopping for groceries when you're hungry. That same advice applies to all shopping. Don't wait until you're desperate and don't shop unless you've got the cash. When you use your credit card and go into debt shopping, you send a message to your child that not controlling money is okay.

What makes a smart consumer? Understanding that what you buy has to be evaluated for more than just comfort or enjoyment.   Quality, usefulness, maintenance cost, and durability need to be factored in when deciding about the price you're willing to pay and whether the item is worth it. Kids are not sophisticated when it comes to understanding the actual value of items.   Value to kids varies with mood, age, and the pressure to buy. Most items have an intrinsic value and a market value. Teaching kids comparison shopping helps them learn about market value.

"Ere you consult your fancy, consult your purse."

— Benjamin Franklin

Understanding market value prepares children for the next principle of consumerism, which is the art of negotiation. Negotiation is a life skill as well as a shopping skill. When shopping, time, convenience, and service are all negotiable, as well as the price, and need to be considered when deciding if you're getting a fair value for something you want. Remind kids to always keep the sales receipt for things they buy in case of repairs or returns.

Learning to contribute to one's community, whether local or global, is an important part of learning the responsibility we all have for the world we live in.

The Gift of Giving

Giving is another aspect of spending that makes us feel good in a different way. Learning to contribute to one's community, whether local or global, is an important part of learning the responsibility we all have for the world we live in.

Surplus wealth is a sacred trust which its possessor is bound to administer in his lifetime for the good of the community.

— Andrew Carnegie

We are lucky to live in the most prosperous country in the world. Most of us share a high standard of living unprecedented in history. But there are still many in need. More so now than previously because the government and corporations are cutting back on social services, medical support, environmental protection, and cultural support.

Children learn about generosity and being charitable from watching their parents, just as they learn about spending. Most people are innately generous. We care about our fellow humans and we care about causes that affect us all. Kids are the same. They have dreams and ideals and they have heart. Many children feel strongly about helping animals, whether it's the Dumb Friends League or helping to save endangered species or saving the dolphins. They worry about war and like to contribute toward world peace. They're compassionate about people who are less fortunate like the homeless or children with incurable diseases. Most kids shopping at Christmas will put their pennies in the Salvation Army kettle.

"Children have never been very good at listening to their elders, but they have never failed to imitate them."

— James Baldwin
(Author)

Children who hear their parents discussing social issues, or doing something about them will develop a social consciousness of their own. They learn most easily by example. Parents enthusiasm and demonstrable support such as belonging and participating in a charity organization, will guide children in the same direction. Enthusiasm is contagious. Children can also join youth groups in their church or school or community which are dedicated to worthy causes. Working towards something good with their peers is very rewarding.

Children who hear their parents discussing social issues, or doing something about them will develop a social consciousness of their own.

The Art of Giving

Children should be committed to using a portion of their spending money for giving. The giving money should only be given away to charities or other organizations or events that benefit others. It is up to each family to decide how this money is given away and how often. I suggest giving the money away at least monthly, but preferably weekly.

The amount or percent of your children's spending money that is to be given away is also between you and your children. A standard guideline is 10% of their spending money. A 10-year-old receiving a $10 weekly allowance would contribute $1 of that each week to a worthy cause.

Causes that attract kids into giving include saving the rain forest, the zoo, adopting children in other countries for $20 or $30 a month which provides food and shelter and clothing, and helping the homeless. Your kids might want to support the local PBS TV station or public radio station. Most families who attend services contribute to the support of the church or synagogue or mosque and the charities they support.

If it's important to you, you can direct your kids toward the charities that you support. Kids also learn a lot when you help them identify causes that interest them to support. Another way of giving is by volunteering time or efforts for an organization — maybe it's picking up trash on the highway or helping to clear hiking trails. They can also collect and donate goods, canned food, blankets, or clothing. They don't have to do their giving in the form of money. They can convert it to goods, or transportation, or postage, or supplies to make something that contributes in another way.

Causes that attract kids into giving include saving the rain forest, the zoo, adopting children in other countries for $20 or $30 a month, which provides food and shelter and clothing, and helping the homeless.

"If there be any truer measure of a man than by what he does, it must be by what he gives."

— Robert South

One thing to be cautious about is if your child starts giving gifts or money in attempt to win affection, friendship, control, attention, or love. Kids can become overly generous. This is just as much of a problem for a child as spending too much. Some children learn early that money can be used to control others. This develops when the child feels powerless in other aspects of his life. Try letting them make more decisions about themselves and their lives on their own. Kids can be competitive in their giving, feeling the more they give, the more praise they'll get. This is a situation in which to remind a child that the thought does count as much as the size or cost of the gift.

Children love to participate and help with meaningful causes. They are almost all generous and sympathetic by nature. Our culture associates giving with money and that can often frustrate kids who don't have a lot of it. On the other hand, they have to be taught how to share with or spend on others. These are not innate behaviors. In order to learn these skills, children have to feel secure and loved in order to be able to let go of material things that provide comfort.

One thing to be cautious about is if your child starts giving gifts or money in attempt to win affection, friendship, control, attention, or love.

Resources

Books

150 Ways Teens Can Make A Difference, by Marian Salzman (Peterson's Guides, 1991).

The Buck Book — All Sorts Of Things You Can Do With A Dollar Bill Besides Spend It, by Anne Akers Johnson (Klutz Press, 1993).

Every Kid's Guide To Intelligent Spending, by Joy Berry (Children's Press, 1988).

The Money Book: A Kid's Guide To Savvy Saving And Spending, by Elaine Wyatt and Stan Hinden (Tambourine Books, 1991).

Simple Ways To Help Your Kids Become Dollar-Smart, by Elizabeth Lewin, C.C.P., and Bernard Ryan, Jr. (Walker And Company, 1994).

Special Events From A To Z: The Complete Educator's Handbook, by Gayle Jasso (Corwin Press, 1996). Ch 7 "Community Service and Volunteer Projects."

Internet

CCCS — Kids and Money
http://www.powersource.com/powersource/cccs/edu/cccscam.html

Kids & Money
http://www.kiplinger.com/drt/drthome.html

Kids' Money
http://pages.prodigy.com/kidsmoney

Money: Kids & Cash
http://www.school.discovery.com/catalog/mon-eykids.html

Software

The Little Shoppers Kit (ages 6-9)
Apple
Tom Snyder Productions, Cambridge, MA
1-800-342-0236

Be a Smart Shopper (ages 11-14)
Apple II series or TRS-80 (51/4" disk)
Victoria Learning Systems, Fairfield, CT
1-800-232-2224

Chapter 11

Saving For A Rainy Day

Saving money regularly can make you rich. As a broker, my biggest clients, the ones who had the most investable money, were not the ones who won the lottery and they were not the ones who inherited it. In fact, those people seem to have more money management problems. One client who inherited money and a business after his father died ended up in jail for drug dealing within a year of his inheritance and managed to squander every dime of it. The people who were successful were the ones who never necessarily made a lot of money (they might have worked for the government for 30 years) but they saved a regular portion of their money over a period of years and years.

An informal survey of brokers and investment advisors around the country turned up some amazing facts. Of their top ten investing clients, they reported that only about 40% were business owners and 15% inherited their money; but 70% to 100% of their investors, regardless of income source, became wealthy by saving over time.

> "I believe it is essential to teach kids at a young age the methodology of saving on a regular basis and to start as soon as possible."
>
> — Richard J. Bloom
> (Bloom Asset
> Management)

Of their top ten investing clients, they reported that only about 40% were business owners and 15% inherited their money; but 70% to 100% of their investors, regardless of income source, became wealthy by saving over time.

Saving is the second component of the Four-Part Money Management System for children. Savings represent the one third of your children's allowance that they need to accumulate over time and think about before spending. For children, saving is a form of deferred spending for large ticket items.

Adults often maintain their savings accounts, not just as a place to accumulate funds for large expenses like a special vacation, but also as a resource to pay for emergencies such as an accident or a hospitalization, and for unplanned expenses like paying for a child's wedding. The reasons most people save fall into four categories:

- Long-term needs: retirement
- Short-term needs: college, house, car
- Emergencies: medical, fire
- Short-term wants: new living room furniture

Children don't need to be concerned with paying for potential emergencies or big events, but it helps them establish an important life-long habit if you teach them early how to save. The younger they are, the easier it is to break old habits and establish new patterns. You'll be doing your kids a lifetime favor by helping them to save regularly.

"Hoarding is not a love of saving but usually a fear of spending. "Don't let your child become too fearful about financial security. Make sure they spend some of it regularly. At the same time, don't get in the habit of bailing your kid out if she overspends regularly. It encourages financial dependence. Hold your child responsible for her own excesses."

— Neale Godfrey

The key to saving for younger kids is learning about deferring gratification, which is putting off satisfaction, not denying it.

At all ages, many of the things children want cost more than they can afford with their weekly spending money. As discussed in Chapter 12, children easily confuse needs and wants. Most of what they want feels urgent and is categorized as a need. It might be a pet gerbil or a pair of inline skates or a light for their bicycle, and for older teens, possibly a car.

The key to saving for younger kids is learning about deferring gratification, which is putting off satisfaction, not denying it. They need to learn how to figure out their priorities, what they want or need now and what can wait. Kids' attention often wanders. Halfway to their goal they may realize they want something else instead. Saving is useful because it allows kids to change their minds as often as they like before committing their money. Having control of savings gives children a feeling of control of their life in general.

To help kids work into the concept of goal setting, help them identify short-term, rewarding savings goals to start — something that can be saved for in one or two weeks. Then stretch it a little longer, and so on. A see-through piggy bank or jar to keep their savings in can help. The child can visually see the money accumulating. Don't use a piggy bank that has to be broken. A reusable one is better. If saving for more than one item, have a bank or container for each and decide what percent of savings go into each account. Work out in advance the time it will take to save for the goal so your child can count off the time.

It helps kids learn to save if they start out with a reachable, tangible goal. Twenty dollars for a new video game; $16 for the CD by the Floating Zebras; $60 for a new pair of basketball shoes; $15 for a light or bell for their bike. For younger kids, it helps to find a picture of what they want in a magazine or catalog and cut it out. You might want to help them keep a written record of what's in their savings account from week to week so they can see their progress towards the coveted item. Rewards that are waited for often are more enjoyable because of the anticipation, like Christmas.

> It helps kids learn to save if they start out with a reachable, tangible goal.

One way to help your kids understand savings goals is to explain the differences between wishes, goals, and plans.

It's not easy for kids to wait to accumulate enough money for something expensive. They see you withdrawing cash from the ATM or using your credit card to get what you want now and don't understand why they have to wait to get what they want. Tell your kids what you are saving for. Probably some is for emergencies, but if there is something concrete, tell them, and show them your gratification when you finally purchase it and bring it home, like a new outfit or a tool for your workshop.

One way to help your kids understand savings goals is to explain the differences between wishes, goals, and plans. A plan is what turns a wish into a goal. A goal is your target, the specific thing you're aiming for. A plan is the list of things you need to do to reach your goal. Wishes are just anything you want. Wanting to own a copy of every single video there is in the world is a wish that will always be a wish. It can't happen so it can't be a goal. Wanting a video of every movie Brad Pitt has made is a wish that can be a goal, but is a pretty hard goal to reach on a kid's budget. Wanting a video of Brad Pitt's most recent movie is a reachable goal. If the video costs $24.00, your child's plan will consist of saving $3 a week for eight weeks, or $6 a week for four weeks, or however much she can afford, until she has saved enough. Goals are just wishes, "I want a video," until they're specific, "I want the Brad Pitt *Seven Years in Tibet* video."

Age seven to 12 is a good time to teach your children how to save, as well as how to cope with spending mistakes. Kids really start being able to save, and to understand the concept of saving, around age eight. If your child wants to save $20 for a poorly constructed toy that you know will inevitably break, let him. After the toy breaks, then show him why the toy wasn't worth it and say that you won't replace it but you will help with a better decision next time.

It depends on your child's age and amount of allowance whether to keep savings in a piggy bank or to deposit in real bank account. Set up a savings schedule for transferring money from the home piggy bank to the bank, maybe whenever $10 to $25 is accumulated at home.

Banking

One way you can prevent your children from looting the third that is the savings portion of their allowance is by making regular trips to the bank with them. A bank protects their money from fire and theft and other accidents at home and keeps the money away from temptation.

Next time you go to the bank, bring the kids along and explain some of the principles of banking like when and why you use your ATM card as opposed to cash or a check. Let your children know that the ATM machine isn't printing greenbacks and the teller isn't giving you money because he likes your signature. The money is being withdrawn from your own account. When your children deposit and withdraw funds from their account, explain that it will mean they have more or less of their own money in the bank, depending on the transaction.

"Saving really helps kids band the connection between how money accumulates
and what it can buy. Think of it as
deferred spending."

— Pat Estess
(author)

Kids love going to the bank, it's an adventure.
Explain banking basics before the first visit and help
your child prepare a list of questions about savings
accounts:

- How much is needed to open an account?
- What interest rate does the bank pay on savings
  accounts?
- How often is the interest compounded?
- How soon does interest start on deposits
- Are there any conditions about withdrawals?
- Are there any banking fees?
- Are they required to maintain a minimum bal-
  ance?

Savings accounts allow the depositor to withdraw money at any time, but many banks charge a
fee if you make more than a certain number of withdrawals a month.

Help your child open a savings account in a bank
sometime between ages six and 10. Money in a bank
is safe, insured by FDIC (Federal Deposit Insurance
Corporation), FSLIC (Federal Savings and Loan
Insurance Corporation), and the National Credit
Union Share Insurance Fund.

The U.S. has the lowest savings rate of any industrialized nation. Americans save 5% of their income, Japanese 10%, and Taiwanese twenty percent. The more you save, the better off you will be in the future.

A Texas A & M University study reported kids have $6 billion in savings.

Help your child open a savings account in a bank sometime between ages six and 10.

More and more banks are starting programs to attract young savers. Some banks offer young customers check writing privileges, automated teller machine (ATM) cards, credit cards, and loans for college or to start their own business, the full range of services offered to adults. My nine-year-old getting cash from an ATM! The thought would cause most parents to shudder. Don't worry, these programs for young customers require active parent oversight.

Many communities around the country have banks with programs that cater to young people. The Mid-America Federal Savings Bank in Clarendon Hills, Illinois has a branch staffed by students in the local high school. The Young Americans Bank in Denver, Colorado lets kids open a savings account with as little as a $10 deposit. When the First National Bank of Pulsar, Tennessee rolled out a club for kids to open a bank account, nearly 500 youngsters showed up with their piggy banks. And in a school saving program sponsored by Dollar Dry Dock Bank in New York, more than 8,000 kids from

When the First National Bank of Pulsar, Tennessee rolled out a club for kids to open a bank account, nearly 500 youngsters showed up with their piggy banks.

kindergarten to eighth grade have saved almost a million dollars since the program began in 1992.

The school PTA sponsors a saving program for kids called Save for America. About half the states participate. The PTA collects your kid's savings once a week, records each amount on a computer, and deposits the money in a sponsoring bank.

If the banks in your area haven't caught on that teaching kids about money management is an important community service, and that kids represent an enormous customer pool, try establishing a family bank at home that works on the same principles, or put your kids' money in your savings account and keep separate records, being sure to pay them the same interest rate. If you keep the money in a "home bank" add the interest to the cash at regular intervals. If you pool your kids savings or set up a bank at home, create some deposit and withdrawal slips for them to access their money, and give them a statement of their transactions and interest earned on a regular basis.

"The safest way to double your money is to fold it over once and put it in your pocket."

— Kin Hubbard

Discipline is the key to successful saving. Follow the rules of the System and they'll be well on their way to learning how to manage money — certainly no small feat. Stray from the guidelines and your kids are liable to be opening up a can of worms instead of a bank account. Just remember, it's okay to laugh all the way to the bank. Just tell your child not to be too obvious about it. Banks offer several forms of savings accounts:

Passbook Savings Account

The bank issues the depositor a passbook in which the bank records all deposits, withdrawals and interest, usually quarterly. Some banks send out a monthly statement instead.

If your bank issues statements instead of a passbook, help your children make their own passbook and make the entries from the statements, or set up a file for the statements or some method of keeping track of their financial transactions.

U.S. Savings Bonds

They're safe and can be bought for a minimum of $25. They can be cashed anytime after six months. If you hold them five years or more, they're guaranteed to pay at least 4% annually. The interest rates are reset every six months. For longer term savings, there are Series EE Savings Bonds which pay double the face value when the bond matures.

Money Market Account

These require a large opening balance and are not insured, but are considered safe. They pay a slightly higher rate of interest than a savings account.

Certificate Of Deposit
(the other kind of "CD")

These are available in six month, one year, or five year intervals. The interest rate is locked in when you buy it. Rates vary daily and among banks. There's a penalty for cashing it in before it comes due.

Explaining Interest

Children are curious about where the bank gets the money to pay them interest on their savings accounts. Explain that the bank lends your money to other people to buy houses, businesses, cars, etc. and charges the borrowers a fee called "interest" and then gives you a percent of that interest as your fee for lending your money to the bank. Typical interest on a savings account is 4% to 5% a year. At 5%, $100 becomes $105 in a year, and $1,000 becomes $1,050. If you save $100 a year for 10 years at 5%, you'll have $1,320.83. A bank savings account is a low-risk investment because it is insured by the Federal Government (FDIC).

Interest can be simple or compound. Simple interest is paid at the end of the year. Compound interest pays on the principal, the original deposit, and on the interest that's accumulating on the principal. Compound interest can be computed yearly, quarterly, monthly, or daily. The shorter the interval, the more interest you're receiving.

Doubling Your Money:
If you divide the number 72 by any given annual interest rate, it will tell you how many years it will take for your money to double. For example, if you deposit $100 in a savings account at 4% interest ($72 \div 4 = 18$), it would take 18 years for your $100 to grow to $200.

Children often lend money to each other. It may be helpful to demonstrate to your child that money loaned to friends isn't making any interest.

Compound interest pays on the principal, the original deposit, and on the interest that's accumulating on the principal.

Saving for College

Saving for college is often an important goal for a child. Seventeen years from now, when your new baby is ready for college, the cost of four years of education at a public university will be approximately $73,100, and at a private school, $186,300. These costs assume a 6% college tuition inflation rate as determined by The College Board.

Regular savings is an important discipline that should be part of your college savings strategy. Decide on an amount you can afford each month or quarter that moves toward your goals and invest the same amount each period.

The fuel that makes money grow is time. The sooner you start investing the more money you can potentially accumulate. For example, if you invest $100 a month and get a 12% annual return, you will have $8,249 at the end of five years, but you will have $66,792 at the end of 17 years.

Start evaluating financial limits on college at least by junior high school and decide what will be expected from your child. Set up a matching college savings fund. If you are saving for his college education he'll be motivated to do the same because you're sending the message that education is important enough to save for.

Resources

Books

A Penney Saved: Teaching Your Children The Values And Life Skills They Will Need To Live In The Real World, by Neale S. Godfrey (Simon & Schuster, 1996).

Kids' Money Journal available from Kids' Money Internet Web site
http://pages.prodigy.com/kidsmoney

Money And Banking, by Lois Canwell (Franklin Watts, 1984).

Magazines

Kids' Money Journal from Kids' Money Internet Web site
http://wc1.webcrawler.com/select/parent.12.html

Internet

Mercantile Bank Lawrence
http://www.mercantilebank.com/lawrence/clubkids/clubinfo.html

Banks

Young Americans Bank
A Denver bank serving kids and young adults up to age 22. Can bank by mail if don't live in the area.
311 Steele St., Denver, CO 80206; 303-321-2265.

Information by Phone

1-800-US-BONDS (1-800-872-6637)
to get the current rate of interest being paid on savings bonds.

Programs

Save for America
Sponsored by PTAs and participating banksin 25 states . For information or to start a program in your school. 4095 173rd Place SE, Bellvue, WA 98008; 206-746-0331

Chapter 12

The Risks And
Rewards Of Investing

Investing is the final component of the Four-Part
Money Management System and is one of the most
important concepts you can teach your child. If you
do well here, investing can positively change the
entire financial future of your child. If your kids do
not have some money put away in investments, they
won't be prepared when something unexpected happens or when a costly opportunity rises. Investing is
a way to prepare for and assure a better future.

Americans, as a rule, do a poor job of investing.
I believe that they do a poor job simply because they
were never taught good sound investment principals
as children. Parents say, "I don't even understand
investing and you're expecting my kids to invest."
Believe it or not, they're ready to learn this lesson in
life; they're ready to learn about business and
finance and the economy. And the way they learn is,
again, by practical, hands-on experience.

When I teach a classroom of 25 kids, I start out by asking, "Does anybody know how to spend money?" Oh, yeah, yeah. They all do. "Does anybody know how to save money?" Oh, yeah, sure. "Anybody know how to give it away?" Yeah. "Anybody know how to invest it?" Silence, nobody raises their hand. They haven't even been introduced to the general concept of investing, much less the how-to.

Investing is simply putting money away that you're not going to spend. That's how you create wealth. What a novel concept. It's also how you create the American dream, accumulating money that you don't actually spend. When you invest in stocks or mutual funds or real estate or buying a business or even an education, you're just transforming a monetary investment into another form of lasting wealth, transferring the wealth from one place to another, but the wealth doesn't go away. When you buy a car, the wealth goes away because the car depreciates. It's worth less when you sell it than when you bought it. It's worth less as soon as you drive it out of the car dealership. Furniture depreciates, computers depreciate. Few children have ever heard of the concept of wealth not going away. If you can teach them that a portion of their money can and should be invested, in other words, treat it in such a way that it won't go away, then over time that money will grow. That's the value of investing. Money that's invested not only doesn't go away, it works for you by growing into greater worth. Understanding that is a tool that kids can use.

The notion of money "working" may seem strange to kids. If you leave money for months and months in a piggy bank or stuff it under the mattress, it's not doing anything but collecting dust. If, however, you put it in a savings account or other finan-

> Money that's invested not only doesn't go away, it works for you by growing into greater worth. Understanding that is a tool that kids can use.

cial product, the bank or company actually pays you for the use of your money.

How to Get Children Started Investing

Start your children investing as early as possible. Realistically, they're probably not ready till about age seven and it may take longer before they have a real grasp of what they're doing. Prior to that you can just put their investment money in a savings account at a bank.

Investing can be a challenge for young people because the rewards seem so far away. We're talking about leaving money undisturbed for ten or twenty years, maybe even longer.

"If I can give one piece of advice to a child regarding investing, my advice would be to start as soon as possible and do it on a regular basis."

— Richard J. Bloom
(Bloom Asset Management)

A third of all the money your child receives in the form of allowance, gifts, or working income — money from any source — should be put aside for investing. The investing component of the child's piggy bank should be emptied every few months — whenever there are sufficient funds with which to buy stock or add to a mutual fund. Take money out of the investment piggy bank quarterly to invest — at the very least, once a year.

Investing can be a challenge for young people because the rewards seem so far away. We're talking about leaving money undisturbed for 10 or 20 years, maybe even longer. It's their money and it's not going to be spent for a long, long time. To a child, Christmas or Hanukkah or their next birthday is a long way away. Depending on age, next week might seem remote. To a child, a very long time is approximately synonymous with never so you will need to explain this several times. The concept is a challenge for kids because the rewards are so far away, 10 or 20 years, and have nothing to do with their life as they know it in childhood. Talk about delayed gratification. Explaining investing to a younger child may take the form of setting down a rule rather than really explaining.

"A third of your money, your investment money, is going to be put away. You are not going to understand what we are doing with it. The money will be locked up and you won't be able to get to it, but it is going to grow and you are going to do what we call "invest it" for things a long, long time from now that you can't even imagine yet. Over time you will learn what investing is about, but those are the rules no matter what."

One good way to deal with the remoteness of the gratification is to make the actual investing fun, an end in itself. As your children mature, the best way to help them understand the concept of investing is to get them involved in the process. Let your children pick their own stocks to invest their money in. Children like buying stocks in companies they know and whose products they use or recognize. They might select something like Microsoft because children use the company software on their computers;

Kids are amazing at ferreting out companies that are doing well and buying stocks in those companies because kids see things for what they are, while parents often get confused with strategy or the details.

or maybe they'll choose Disney or McDonald's or Nike. Kids are amazing at ferreting out companies that are doing well and buying stocks in those companies because kids see things for what they are, while parents often get confused with strategy or the details. Kids know the products they use, they know what's hot, they know what's not, and they usually invest in products that, over the long term, are good investments. But don't get too detailed with them or go overboard with this investing thing. They'll learn it. They'll pick it up over time. If they own shares of Wal-Mart and you go into a Wal-Mart and they walk around they'll realize, "Hey, I own a little piece of this," and then they might decide they like Target better so they want to sell their Wal-Mart and buy Target. And it's amazing how one share of this and then two shares of that and a savings account accumulate and all their investments start to pile up, and that's when kids really see the value of the growth of money.

They may not completely understand the concept of investing. That's okay. But they may get curious enough to look up various stock quotes in the paper. Encourage them to do that, to watch their stock, watch it go up and down, and to understand why. And they'll start putting two and two together. Kids will really learn by doing. After some experience, you'll notice that your children even start to develop their own philosophy of investing. They'll receive the annual report, they'll get the quarterly reports, they'll get updates, they'll get dividend checks from the company, and they'll start to see — experience — their money growing rather than just getting a boring bank statement once a quarter. And sometimes their investments will go down in value, too. But that's part of the experience.

"And gain is gain, however small."

— Robert Browning

You don't need to over-emphasize the investing concept. About once a year, maybe on your children's birthdays, help them review their investments for the year. Have them take a really hard look and ask themselves, "Do I like what I'm doing? Do I not like it? What's worked? What hasn't? Do I want to make any changes in my investments." Your kids will pick this up on their own.

Encourage them to do that, to watch their stock, watch it go up and down, and to understand why.

"Too many people suffer from financial illiteracy. They need to learn how to do a better job of investing if they want to invest at all . . . . They don't do a good job of investing because they haven't taken the time to learn about finances. It's a matter of research. Of reading company reports, looking at what makes a company tick. They will do all of this research for things, but they'll hear a tip (about a company) on the bus and put $10,000 on a stock. That's not investing, that's gambling . . . . When money is invested, it can help a company grow, and that in turn helps the country."

— Peter Lynch
(manager of Fidelity
Investment's
Magellan Fund)

My kids look at their stocks all the time, and they talk about them. It's strange. It really is. It's weird. I hear my kids talking about their stocks. That's funny to me. You know when I was a kid we got bored at Christmas and Thanksgiving dinners because we weren't included when the adults were talking about grownup things. My nine-year-old and 12-year-old now have conversations between themselves about the product lines of this and that company they own. I hear, "I'm going to sell my stock. It's lousy," and "It's cruddy. I'm switching companies." They get into it. And that's how kids learn about investing.

An understanding of investing is one of the most valuable concepts that you can teach your children. You're basically showing them how to set aside a portion of their money forever that will continue to increase. The key here is to focus on offering the kids the ability to make choices and making sure they understand what they're getting involved in, and then letting them experiment and experience it for themselves. From investing, your children will learn about the economy, they'll learn about stocks, and they'll learn about business in general so that some day when they're in the business world, they will have a little better grasp of how business works.

My nine-year-old and 12-year-old now have conversations between themselves about the product lines of this and that company they own.

That's why kids have done pretty well with investing over the years and why I encourage kids to invest.

Types of Investments

Explain to your children the difference between money they save and money they invest. Savings is the way for them to accumulate enough money to buy things that cost from about $10 to several hundred or $1000. Investing is done over a long period of time and is the way to accumulate enough money for one-time very expensive things like college or a house or a wedding or even retirement, things that cost many thousands of dollars.

Not all big purchases count as an investment. Some, like cars, start to lose value as soon as they're bought. They depreciate, meaning you can't sell it for as much or more than you bought it for. A house, on the other hand, usually appreciates; it grows in value over time. Other types of tangible property that appreciate and are investments are stamp or coin or art collections — even sports trading cards.

Some forms of investment aren't tangible. An investment can also be defined in terms of one's time and purpose. For example, a good education is a form of investment because it allows an individual a fuller, richer life. On balance, college graduates earn a lot more money than people who only finish highschool. And highschool graduates tend to earn more than students who drop out. There are exceptions, but very few. A college education is an investment that increases one's worth, just like a monetary investment.

The key here is to focus on offering the kids the ability to make choices and making sure they understand what they're getting involved in, and then letting them experiment and experience it for themselves.

An invest-
ment can
also be
defined in
terms of
one's time
and purpose.

"The one ingredient that I believe is essential for the success of an investor is goals and objectives. In other words, I believe an investor cannot be successful unless they truly understand why they are investing their money."

— Richard J. Bloom

If
Christopher
Columbus
had invested
one dollar in
the New
World Bank
when he
arrived here
in 1492, at a
5% interest
rate, how
much money
would he
have today?

A portfolio is a group of investments. A typical family portfolio might consist of a house, a business, some land, a savings account, some stocks or mutual funds, and a pension fund or personal retirement account.

There are two main elements working together that make money grow: time and the rate of interest. And guess what your kids' greatest asset is right now? It's their time. They have a lot of years ahead of them. If you can get them started investing now, the time will have the most value over the long haul. A third element that affects the rate at which invested money will grow is the interval at which the interest is compounded. If Christopher Columbus had invested one dollar in the New World Bank when he arrived here in 1492, at a 5% interest rate, how much money would he have today? Would the answer be $42 thousand dollars? No. $42 million dollars? No. The answer is $42 billion dollars. Columbus' one dollar would have grown to $42 billion dollars between 1492 and 1998. That's the value of compounding interest and the value of time. Now we all don't have hundreds of years, but our kids have a lot more of it than we adults do, and time is the one thing that makes money grow the most. It's not the rate of interest. It's the time over which your money is invested.

There are not a lot of options for savings besides putting the money in a bank account. Savings represents money you plan on withdrawing in the foreseeable future so it needs to be easily accessible. Investments, because the money is put away for a long time, offer many more opportunities for your money to work for you. But most investments do come with a certain amount of risk. Risk is the chance that your investment may lose money in the short term. Not a happy prospect. But the risk is balanced because a good investment is more likely to earn a lot more money than a savings account over the long term. Smart investing means balancing risks and rewards.

Here's your choices for investing. You can leave it in the piggy bank with a lock on it and you earn zero percent interest, but you also have zero risk unless the house burns down and your money burns up. The second choice, the next safest choice, would be buying a government bond or putting it in a bank savings account. Encourage your children to choose how to invest their money and to decide what level of risk they want to take with their money.

Are your children willing to invest $50 in a stock and watch it go down to $40 or $35 with the chance that it might go up to $100 and double their money? Or are they more interested in investing their $50 dollars in something less risky, watch it march up slowly, and know it will be worth $50.14 next quarter. The general rule is that the risk and the potential reward from an investment go up or down together. For example, a savings account has the lowest investment risk. It's insured by the government so you get your investment back no matter what, and

The answer is $42 billion dollars.

the interest rate is guaranteed, but it offers the lowest interest rate or rate of return of any investment. Stocks are probably the most fun to invest in, and they offer the most potential return, about 10% on a good stock. But the risk you take is also the highest for any form of investment. With stocks, it's not only possible that your rate of return will decrease, it's also possible to lose your initial investment, although you can't lose more than you've put in.

If kids are going to try out different levels of risk, which is probably what they're going to end up doing, set an evaluation period every quarter or biannually for them to reassess the risks and the payoffs; to evaluate the investment and see where they're comfortable. They might love it, they might hate it, but it gives them the opportunity of changing their mind and their risk comfort level.

INVESTMENT/SAVINGS RISK REWARD CHART

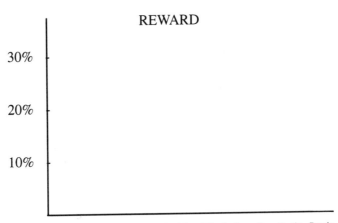

Some different forms of investments:

- Savings account
- Stocks
- Bonds
- Mutual funds
- Stock options
- Commodities
- Precious metals (gold, silver)
- Futures
- U.S. Government securities
- Certificates of deposit (CDs)
- Municipal securities
- Marketable debt securities
- Equity securities
- Foreign securities
- Money market securities
- Banker's acceptances
- Commercial paper
- Real estate

[The most common of these are explained in depth in Chapter 13]

* * *

When your children own stocks or mutual funds, they will often receive quarterly checks in the mail with the dividends the company pays on their investment. As part of the Four-Part Money Management System, don't let your kids treat that money as income. It should not be divided into thirds like

other income. If you are investing and the investments have rewards to them such as dividends or
interest payments, then that money should be reinvested back into the same company or into other
companies so that it can grow and accumulate.
Otherwise, if they keep bleeding the investment for
its earnings, it will never have a chance to grow and
be worth substantial amounts later on.

The next chapter explains in detail about the different kinds of investments your kids can make and
how to get the information they need to make decisions about investing.

Resources

Books

The Kids' Money Book, by Neale S. Godfrey (Checkerboard, 1991).

Kiplinger's Money-Smart Kids: And Parents Too, Ch. 7 "Raise a Wall St. Whiz Kid," by Janet Bodnar (Kiplinger Books, 1995).

Games

The Stock Market Game
Securities Industry Foundation for Economic Education
120 Broadway, 35th Floor
New York, NY 10271-0280
212-608-1500 Fax 212-732-6096
e-mail gtalamas@sia.com

Download Money-Tration
(a version of Concentration)
http://www.younginvstor.com/Moneytration.html

Chapter 13

Investing In Independence

There are a number of options available for long-term investing. It's fine to shift investable money between investments, but remember that money shouldn't be cashed out of investments for 10 or 20 years or even longer. The more time invested money stays put, the more it will grow and benefit your children. In the world of investing, time makes money grow.

You, as the parent will need to carefully oversee your children's investments and you will have to make the investments for them since they are minors. Unless you are already a sophisticated investor yourself, you will want to consult a banker, financial advisor, or stockbroker before investing your children's money.

If you are investing, you can consider registering some shares in your child's name when you are buying a number of shares for yourself. Or you can consult with your broker about opening a custodial account for your children. The legal and financial ramifications of these options are discussed in depth in Chapter 15.

Most full-service stockbrokers charge a commission which can be as high as $100, even to purchase a single share of stock. To reduce the fees or commissions, there are discount brokerage firms, and brokerless alternatives such as investment newsletters, and investment co-ops in which members buy and sell shares from other members, or you can buy stock directly from the company.

One way to purchase stock in a company for as little as $25 is to be enrolled in a company's Dividend Reinvestment Plan commonly called a DRIP. DRIPs are plans offered by companies for the reinvestment of cash dividends by purchasing additional shares or fractional shares on the dividend payment date. Many DRIPs also allow the investment of additional cash from the shareholder, known as an Optional Cash Payment or Optional Cash Purchase (OCP). The DRIP is usually administered by the company without charge, or with just a nominal fee to the participants, and many allow additional purchases of as little as $10 to $25. For most DRIPs you must already be a shareholder of the company to enroll and must own a minimum of one stock, but some require more shares.

Stocks that companies offer directly for sale to the investing public are sometimes referred to as No-Load Stocks. These stocks can be purchased directly from the company without using a broker or paying brokerage commissions. To find out if a company offers its stock for sale directly, and if it has a DRIP, call the company's Investor Relations dept. You can find the various company phone numbers and addresses in your local library's business directories or by searching for the company on the Internet.

One way to purchase stock in a company for as little as $25 is to be enrolled in a company's Dividend Reinvestment Plan, commonly called a DRIP.

Stocks that companies offer directly for sale to the investing public are sometimes referred to as No-Load Stocks.

Types of Investments

An investment is a place to park your money with someone who will use it and pay you for using it. Banks use the money invested in your savings account to make loans and then pay you back in the form of interest. A safe and easy way to start your child investing is through banks which offer some low risk investment "products" such as savings accounts, money-market accounts, and certificates of deposit. The investments are safe because they are ensured by the Federal Government, so if the bank is robbed or burns down, the money is still safe.

An invest-ment is a place to park your money with some-one who will use it and pay you for using it.

Money-Market Accounts

Money-market accounts pay higher interest rates than normal savings accounts, but they also require higher minimums of deposit and have stricter rules governing how often a customer may make a with-drawal. Money-market accounts can be purchased at most banks.

Certificates of Deposit (CDs)

A CD is purchased for a set amount, usually a mini-mum, and for a set amount of time: a month, a year, five years. The advantage is that CDs pay an even higher rate of interest than money-market accounts. But CDs cannot be "invaded." In other words, there are financial penalties for cashing out a CD before its "maturity." They can be purchased through many banks.

The next level of investing, and somewhat riskier, includes stocks and mutual funds. About 10% of children progress from savings accounts and bank products to investing in stocks and mutual funds by the age of 11 or 12. Since children cannot make their own investments, you need to do it for them. To make an investment for your child, convert your child's investment money into a check, cashiers check, or money order. Before investing, it is very important to call the companies or mutual funds you are interested in and ask for an annual report or prospectus.

A standard prospectus gives you current information on:

- Fees
- Investment policies
- Portfolio strategies
- Investment restrictions
- Risks and investment considerations
- How to purchase shares
- How to redeem shares
- Shareholder services
- Net asset value
- Distributions
- Income taxes
- Investment return
- Management of the fund
- Description of shares

Explaining the Stock Market to Your Kids

Stock represents ownership in a publicly traded company. Privately held companies, like some family owned businesses or companies owned by one or a few individuals, may not issue stock. An investor may buy a share of stock which gives him or her part ownership in the company. With stock ownership comes the right to vote on company matters. Stock holders can participate as shareholders by attending a shareholders meeting and addressing the company's executives and Board of Directors.

Individual stocks rise or drop depending upon the number of sellers compared to the number of buyers. Investors decide to buy or sell depending on the past performance of the company or the anticipated future performance. A rise or drop is typically indicated by the change in the total share prices of a select group of stocks such as the Dow Jones Industrial Average (which shows the action of the 30 most actively traded blue-chip stocks on the stock market) or the Standard & Poor 500 (which tracks 500 different stocks of different sizes and may be a better measure of the market). An individual company's stock can rise when the market drops and vice versa. A rise in the overall market represents cumulative optimism and a drop, pessimism, and many see the fluctuations as an indication of good or bad economic times ahead. Daily fluctuations have little value except as a general indication of how the market is doing.

The stock market is like a supermarket. If there are a lot of buyers for shares in a company, the price goes up. If a lot want to sell, the price goes down. The Dow or the S&P 500 represent the average price of that index's stocks. If the index goes down, there were probably more sellers than buyers and vice versa.

Unlike older investors who may need their money in just a few years for retirement, younger investors don't need to worry about the daily or weekly fluctuations in the market because they have

The stock market is like a supermarket. If there are a lot of buyers for shares in a company, the price goes up. If a lot want to sell, the price goes down.

a long time horizon for their investments. They don't need their money back for a long time so their investments have more time to grow.

If your children's money is invested, I think it is important as a family to sit down maybe once a week or once a month and look up the kids' stock quotes. After doing it together five or six times, then the kids will learn how to do it themselves and they can start following the stocks themselves. It makes it fun, it makes it interactive, and all of a sudden investing takes on a life of it own rather than just being a boring old subject like most people think it is.

Before the first investment, teach your kids how to track various stocks. Get the business section of the newspaper and turn to the listings for New York Stock Exchange. Find a stock for a company that your child is familiar with like Disney or McDonald's. Explain that each share of stock listed represents a share of ownership in that company. Explain what the numbers in each column for the stock mean. Have your child pick a stock and track the price of the stock for a week by writing down the daily figures. When you're watching television, point out the stock tickers on CNN and CNBC. Let your child look for the stock he is tracking on the ticker and compare it with the price in the newspaper. Review the stock price changes at the end of the week and explain what they mean, that the price has gone up or down, and compute how much an imaginary share of the stock would have gained or lost in the week. Let your child compute how much profit or loss he would have if he owned a share of that stock.

How To Read A Stock Table

(1) High	(2) Low	(3) Stock	(4) Div.	(5) Yld.	(6) Rat.	(7) 100s	(8) High	(9) Low	(10) Cls	(11) Chg.
48	331/4	AT&Ts	1.32	3.3	12	49859	403/8	393/4	403/8	+3/4
841/4	621/4	Aetnapf	4.76	5.8	248		825/8	815/8	815/8	-11/4

(Two actual NYSE stock entries for Wednesday, February 19, 1997
AT&T Communications and Aetna Insurance Co.)

Columns 1 and 2. "52-w High" and "52-w Low."
These two columns report the highest and lowest prices of a stock during the last 52 weeks. Prices are shown in dollars and fractions of a dollar instead of cents.

1/8 = .12 1/2 cents   3/8 = 37 1/2 cents   5/8 = 62 1/2 cents
7/8 = 87 1/2 cents   1/4 = 25 cents   3/4 = 75 cents

Column 3. "Stock."
This is the abbreviated name of the company issuing the stock.

s — signifies a stock split sometime during the last 52 weeks. A stock split is the division of a stock into a larger number of lower-priced shares. The dividend amount begins with the date of the split.

pf — preferred stock means stocks have preferred treatment and usually pay a fixed dividend which must be paid before common stocks can receive any dividend.

Most stocks listed are common stocks. The more profit a company earns, the more profit there is for common stockholders. If the company loses money, owners of common stock share that loss up to the amount they have invested in the stock. A share of common stock usually allows its owner to vote for the company's Board of Directors.

Column 4. "Div."
This number shows the dividends paid for each share of stock. Dividends are usually paid quarterly. This number is the current quarterly cash dividend multiplied by a 4 to show how much dividend would be paid in a year at this rate. Some companies do not pay dividends.

Column 5. "Yld."

This number is the percentage yield which is the amount of dividends received per share of stock compared with the price of that stock. The yield is calculated by dividing the dividend per share of stock by the closing price (column 10) of the stock and then multiplying by 100 to obtain a percentage.

Column 6. "P-E Rat."

PE stands for price-earnings ratio. This ratio measures how many times greater the stock price is than the earnings per share. The P-E ratio is calculated by dividing the stock's closing price by the earnings per share for the latest year.

Investors often use the P-E ratio to compare a particular company to other businesses in the same industry.

Column 7. "Sales 100s."

This number is the volume of shares traded in hundreds of shares. To compute the actual number of shares traded, multiply the number by 100.

Columns 8 and 9. "High" and "Low."

These report the highest and lowest prices paid for the stock on this particular trading day.

Column 10. "Cls." The closing price or last price shows the price of a share of stock in its last trade at the close of the market on this particular day.

Column 11. "Chg."

This reports any change in the stock's price and is the difference between the last price of a stock on this particular day and the last price on the previous trading day. The amount is preceded by a plus (+) or minus (-) sign to indicate whether the price of the stock went up or down.

Investment Registers

It's important (and fun) for kids to keep track of their investments in some kind of journal or list or investment register which should be updated each time a transaction occurs. All organizations that offer investments send out statements to their investors, usually quarterly, but at least once a year. The information in the register is updated whenever a statement comes in the mail from the bank or mutual fund or broker. Take time to review the statements with your kids and make sure they update their personal register.

A register needs to record initially the name of the company or fund or stock, how many shares are purchased, on what dates, and for what amount. Subsequent entries record dividends paid, whether the income is re-invested, additional investments, and a description of any transactions that occur over the year. There also needs to be an entry for date sold and for what amount. The total of all the entries equals the current value of the total portfolio. The current value of an investment is its current market price, which can be found in the stock tables of the business section of the newspaper or from the financial news or TV or from the Internet. Categories on an investment register include:

- Dates of transactions;
- Description of investment: company name and number of shares purchased;
- Amount paid into the investment when it is purchased;
- Amount cashed out when investment is sold;
- Running total from investments for the year (current value is determined using current market prices for individual investments);

• Dividends or capital gains paid out or re-invested.

The register can also be used to record when a stock "splits" — that is, when the company doubles the number of shares and reduces the price in half (which makes a share more affordable and attracts new investors).

BASIC INVESTMENT REGISTER

Date	Description/# Shares		Deposits	Withdrawals	Total
2/19/97	AT&T	5 shares	$198.75		$198.75
7/20/97	AT&T	2 shares	$96.00		$102.75

The information in the register is also important for tax reasons. Any income from investments is subject to taxation and the profit (the difference between purchase price and selling price) when a stock or mutual fund is sold is subject to capital gains tax.

Stocks that Appeal to Kids

One of the greatest ways to help your kids learn about investing is to let them select companies they use or like or relate to. Help them make a list of products or services that appeal to them and show them how to find the company name on the product or service. Then have them make a list of a half dozen companies whose stock they want to find out about like Nike, Disney, Reebok or Microsoft. Call Shareholder Services for each company, there's usu-

One of the greatest ways to help your kids learn about investing is to let them select companies they use or like or relate to.

ally an 800 number, and ask them to send you an annual report. What you will get in the mail is a beautifully put together book on the company with pictures and all the financial information and how-to investment information all in one document. Take the half dozen or so annual reports and spread them out in front of your child and then let your child dig through them and let them choose which stock they want to invest in. If they're younger, they will probably respond more to the pictures than to the financial information, but that's fine. Over time, they'll learn how to pick stocks in a more technical fashion, but right now its okay to let them experience the process of selecting the stocks themselves, and I can't think of a better way to do it than spreading out annual reports in front of them and letting them choose for themselves.

Types of companies that may appeal to children include:

- Film companies: Lorimar Productions, Disney;
- Gum and candy companies: William Wrigley Jr. Co. sends stockholders a 100-stick box of gum each December;
- Soda companies: Coca Cola;
- Stores where they shop: Target, Wal-Mart, Toys R Us, 7-11, Gap;
- Products they use: video games, athletic shoes, toys, bicycles, skates, cereal; 3M, for a small charge, offers holiday gift boxes of tape, Post-Its and other products;
- Entertainment companies: Disney offers the Magic Kingdom Club with discounts on resorts and theme parks;
- Clothing companies: The Gap, Banana Republic;

- Food companies: Kellogg sends a packet of coupons for goodies like Pop Tarts and Froot Loops.

"Picking a stock is easy if you do the work. If you can't explain to a 10 year old in three minutes or less why you picked a stock, you shouldn't own that stock . . . . There are no formulas. It doesn't make much difference if someone buys on the same day each year of when the market is at its highest or lowest point of the year. The returns will be within 1% of each other."

— Peter Lynch

Mutual Funds

Another option for low minimum investment is a mutual fund. Many can be opened with an investment of as little as $100 or $500. Automatic monthly investments can run as little as $25 a month. Mutual funds are a collection of investments you can buy. The investments are picked by an expert known as a portfolio manager. Stock mutual funds invest primarily in the stock in different companies. When you invest, it's in all the stocks that the mutual fund

Another option for low minimum investment is a mutual fund.

owns so you own little pieces of a whole bunch of different companies. You can get information by contacting the fund company directly or a broker. Always read the fund's prospectus before you invest or send money.

Stocks are among the best performing investments. Stock mutual funds give additional benefits of professional management, diversification, and convenience.

An example of a good mutual fund for children is the Stein Roe Young Investor's Fund. The Stein Roe Young Investor Fund invests in companies that affect the lives of children and teenagers, including Disney, McDonalds, and Coca Cola. You can open the fund for $100. It's designed to be a fun and educational experience for young investors. The Fund provides shareholders with educational materials designed to teach kids about investing. They have low minimums and allow kids to contribute money directly. They send out a quarterly newsletter to the kids, to the shareholders, and they also really believe in teaching kids about money, not just handling the investment. This is not an endorsement for their particular fund. As for any fund or stock, make sure to read the prospectus before investing.

Always read the fund's prospectus before you invest or send money.

Other Investments

As young investors become more savvy, you or your financial advisor may introduce them to other types of investments like bonds, commodities, and precious metals. When the investment is eventually sold, the goal is to sell it for more money than was originally paid for it. For example, if the real estate market is good, most people make a profit when they sell their house.

There are numerous books and other resources that explain the different kinds of investment products in detail.

Resources

Internet

The Art of Investment (articles)
http://www.aofi.com/articles/grenby/

Disney Investor
http://www.disney.com/investors/

Government Services. Investment Professionals. Investment Data.
http://www.aaii.org/iigii.html

http://www.sun.sjen.org

Liberty Financial homepage, Young Investor area
http://www.younginvestor.com/

Motley Fool
(online financial forum for the individual investor)
http://www.fool.com/
Or: on AOL at keyword "Fool"

National Association of Investors Corporation
http://consumer-net.org/resource/cn-NAIC.htm
http://www.wsdinc.com/pgs

Stein Roe Mutual Fund (information for kids)
http://www.younginvestor.com/YI/youngp.html

Stein Roe Mutual Fund parents' site (for Young Investor Fund prospectus)
http://www.younginvestor.com/parents.html
or call 1-800-403-KIDS

Games

Liberty Financial Young Investor Computer Game
(for PC computers)
(risk, income taxes, financial planning, mutual
funds, Wall Street, economy)
1-800-403-KIDS

Low Cost Stocks

First Share
(A $12 membership fee allows you to purchase sin-
gle shares of stocks from other members)
1-800-683-0743

The Low Cost Investment Plan of the National
Association of Investors Corp.
(For a $32 annual fee members can buy shares in any
of 110 companies)
313-543-0512

Moneypaper
(For $72 annual newsletter subscription, readers can
buy shares in stocks mentioned in the current issue
for a $15 fee. Other stocks can be purchased for a
$20 fee)
1-800-592-1551

Chapter 14

Earning The Extras

Work represents a type of barter; trading your time, energy, and physical or mental skill for money which in turn is traded for the things you need and want.

Parents need to help their younger children understand the connection between work and money. If you work out of the house, your kids may not understand that those hours you spend away from home each week have to do with paying the electric bill and whether you can buy them new running shoes this month. The concept would be simpler to grasp if you brought home cash payment from your job each week and personally took that cash to the grocery store and mortgage company and phone company to make your payments. But most workers receive their income in the form of a check or an automatic deposit to a checking account, and they pay their bills the same way. There's nothing tangible for your child to see to make a connection.

It's even more difficult for children to make the link between work and income when parents work in a service-related job rather than producing a concrete product. It will take some creativity on your part to explain successfully to them what you accomplish at your job and what you're getting paid to do. So much of today's work is done by phone, computer, modem, and fax. It's difficult to see the outcome of that work and hard to understand why you get paid for typing and talking on the phone all day.

With the exception of the self-employed, most people work with or for someone. If it's possible, take your children with you to work sometime so they can see what you do "for a living." Introduce them to your boss or manager or employees or co-workers. Walk them through your place of work so they can see how your job fits into the whole process and what the final product or service is.

Unless your children are expecting a large inheritance or trust fund, they will have to work for the money they need to sustain themselves. Working is a large part of every adult life. Help your children prepare for this role in their lives. If you've been following this book, you've shown your children how to manage their money. Now show them how to earn the money to manage.

Like everything else, kids develop their attitudes about work from their parents and other close adults. If parents are always complaining about their job, the boss, the pay, the long hours, kids don't get to see the rewarding aspects of working: the satisfaction and the rewards. They can easily develop a bad attitude long before they ever need to work. Let your children in on the good aspects of your job. Show them your paycheck before you deposit it in the bank. Tell them about the aspects of your job that you find rewarding: the work itself, the salary, your co-workers, security, benefits, career move, whatever you

If parents are always complaining about their job, the boss, the pay, the long hours, kids don't get to see the rewarding aspects of working: the satisfaction and the rewards.

find attractive. When you have a particular success or triumph at work, share that news with your kids. Share the good feelings you get from it. Let them see that work is not all misery and frustration.

Preparing for Work

When they successfully interact with the world, they start having a sense of their own place in it.

Any type of work can help your children tap into their undiscovered skills and grapple with the concept of responsibility. Jobs help to build kids' confidence. When they successfully interact with the world, they start having a sense of their own place in it. Their self-esteem increases with their power to earn and to take care of themselves. A job is the beginning of developing a sense of independence and self-reliance.

"If you're comfortable with the idea of your child walking the neighbor's dog or cutting someone's lawn, by all means give the go-ahead. It can be a boost to a child's self-esteem and sense of responsibility."

— Eve Leppel
(psychologist)

While younger children may not be ready to work on their own or out of the house, you can help them develop some independence and confidence in their abilities if you occasionally hire them to do extra tasks for you that aren't part of their regular chores: repotting plants, washing the car, cleaning out closets. Make sure to differentiate clearly between work they do for you for pay and the unpaid chores which are part of their regular household responsibility as discussed in Chapter 8. Typically, these are jobs parents would do themselves or pay someone else to do: matching socks, cutting grass, painting fences — extra jobs around the house that go beyond chores or normal household responsibilities.

Challenge your kids with a variety of work. They may have hidden abilities you and they don't know about. Do be specific about the task you're assigning because it can mean something different to you and to your child. Cleaning, for example, can mean dusting, washing, organizing, straightening, or throwing away. Make your expectations clear, including what time you expect the job to be finished by, what the specific goal of the task is, and then let your children handle it as they see fit. They may not do it your way, but let them experiment and find a way that works for them within the allotted time.

When your children finish a job, review the work done with your children right away and don't pay them until the work is complete and done to your satisfaction. If they've missed something, caringly show them how to do it properly and let them finish. If you pay them for a shoddy job or unfinished work, they'll never learn. Remember, your appreciation of a job well done is just as important to your children as the money they receive for the work.

If you do "hire" your younger children, pay them by the job, not by the hour. The pace at which kids

Remember, your appreciation of a job well done is just as important to your children as the money they receive for the work.

work varies greatly for different reasons. If they work slowly, it might be because they're dawdling but it could also be that they are being meticulous. Similarly, working quickly may indicate efficiency but it could also mean they are doing a superficial or incomplete job.

Don't pay your children at a discount rate as a cheap source of labor. Give them a fair rate, the same you would pay if you hired out to do the work, but don't overpay either. Let your children help you research what the fair going rate is for the work. It will help them grasp quickly the connection between hard work and spending money.

Another way that younger children can start preparing for the world of work is by volunteering. It not only teaches the kids new skills, but the value of participating in the community and helping those less fortunate. One 11-year-old who loved animals and doctoring signed up for a program though her school that placed her as an assistant to a vet after school for a month, and then as an assistant in a pediatrician's office watching the kids who were waiting to see the doctor. Later, she volunteered as an assistant to an arts and crafts program for younger children. The next summer she volunteered as a candy striper at the local hospital. When she moved up to paying jobs at 13, she baby-sat, did lifting and moving, and clerical work. She promoted her services and, for a year, picked up two children from school for working mothers and took care of them at home until their mothers arrived from work. By the time she looked for her first job in the adult working world at 18, she had already built up an impressive resume of skills, experience, and letters of recommendation.

Volunteering for older kids can take the form of internships. Many smaller businesses are willing to train kids in return for work

Another way that younger children can start preparing for the world of work is by volunteering.

Many younger teenagers find that baby-sitting is a good source of income, especially because of the flexible hours. A good way to prepare your pre-teens for baby-sitting later is for them to work as a mother's helper. This is a job helping the mother of an infant or toddler while the mother is in the house. It's easier for the mother to get things done if there's someone to watch or distract the toddler. Baby sitters are expected to care for children on their own when the parents are out. It's a good idea for any prospective baby sitter to complete the Red Cross Baby Sitting Class which accepts kids 11 and older. Some other ways, as kids grow older, that they can prepare for working are:

- Helping neighbors and relatives: pulling weeds, pet sitting, lawn care, baby sitting;
- Help with parents' work: Most parents' jobs involve some small task their kids can do. Kids are anxious to get involved and generally work hard and do a good job;
- Help with kids' work: Parents can get temporary jobs with the idea that the kids will help with most of the work and earn most of the money: delivering phone directories;
- Kids starting their own business: Provide a service, make their own product, or sell someone else's goods;
- Part-time and summer jobs.

For older kids, part-time entry level jobs include fast food restaurants and retail stores where they can cashier, do inventory, display setup, pricing, and warehousing. These jobs teach the basic good skills they'll need like dealing with customers, getting to work on time, working on a team, and working under pressure at busy times.

Whatever type of work your children choose, it will help them to prepare a resume. Even if they don't have "job" experience, they have skills and traits they've developed at home and school: creative, organized, reliable, good at math, good writer, artistic, athletic, on time, strong. For their resume, they will need two or three personal references who are not family members, such as a teacher, minister, coach, or some other adult who knows them.

Kids need to learn to budget time as well as money.

It is not uncommon for kids' jobs to interfere with school work and family life. Taking time with your child to establish and maintain a balance between the three is essential. Place a limit on your kids time dedicated to outside employment. They still need a balance. Kids need to learn to budget time as well as money.

Legal Considerations

Both Federal and State governments have labor laws which restrict the kind and amount of work that children under 16 are allowed to do. For instance, kids under 14, technically, can only be employed by their parents. There is no law, however, saying your kids cannot be self-employed.

If your kid is an entrepreneur and works alone, there are no restrictions on when or how many hours he works. It gets complicated if your child wants to hire additional manpower. There are government forms and red tape. A free government publication explains what he needs to know about employees. The Handy Reference Guide to the Fair Labor Standards Act from the U.S. Dept. of Labor, 202-209-4907. It's easier to have a partner than to hire help.

Federal law allows kids to work at a number of different types of jobs starting at age 14: Newspaper delivery, acting, non-hazardous farm work, office/clerical, sales, retail.

During the school year, kids under age 14 cannot work: During school hours, before 7 a.m. or after 7 p.m. (except for newspaper delivery), more than three hours a day, more than 18 hours a week.

During the summer kids under age 14 cannot work: After 9 p.m., more than eight hours a day, more than 40 hours a week.

Kids under 16 may not do hazardous work.

If your children want to work, be sure to check your state's laws with the Department of Labor or Office of Employment because state laws concerned with children working vary and are often more restrictive than federal laws.

Some money making activities that appeal to teenagers, like yard work or a food operation, need a license or permit from the city or town government. If your kids are working, they need to have a social security number and may be liable for federal and state income tax. If they operate a business under any other name than their own, they have to register the name with the county clerk's office or possibly the state. If the business is set up as or evolves into anything other than a sole proprietorship, you may need legal and tax advice.

Young Entrepreneurs

Many kids are attracted to entrepreneurial activities from setting up a lemonade stand to starting a dog walking business. Encourage your young entrepreneur. Ten to 11 is a good age for them to start. The benefits are both personal and educational. They'll develop a set of hands-on business skills like planning, researching, competing, marketing, and public relations. They'll also find out about learning from their own mistakes, taking setbacks in stride, and they'll learn the value of responsibility, reliability, honesty, and persistence. They'll discover that these characteristics have tangible benefits.

In the 90s, one third of teens, 12 to 19, work part-time at jobs outside the home on a year-round basis. In 1995, teens collectively earned $90 billion.

Help your kids with their business idea, not by telling them what to do, but by asking them questions that will help them understand what's needed so they can come up with their own solutions.

Help your kids with their business idea, not by telling them what to do, but by asking them questions that will help them understand what's needed so they can come up with their own solutions. Help them brainstorm. A successful business fills a need people have. The best business is one that matches a skill or interest or hobby or talent your child has with a need other people have. Photography, shining shoes, making things, clowning around, magic, cooking, math, music . . . . Every child has some ability. It just takes some imagination to figure out how to market it.

The first step to starting a business is to draw up a business plan. Help your young entrepreneurs do the necessary research and draw up a plan that is realistic. Some of the planning considerations include:

- Start-up costs
- Budget
- Financing
- Location
- Product or service
- Market research
- Overhead costs vs. potential profit
- Setting a price
- Advertising
- Promotion
- Bookkeeping
- Time involved
- Inventory
- Materials needed
- Time management
- Number of clients or customers that can be realistically handled

"Beware of little expenses; a small leak will sink a great ship."

— Benjamin Franklin

Like adults, many kids overextend themselves in their initial enthusiasm for a new enterprise. Undercapitalization, short cash flow, and not being able to deliver as promised are three common areas. If your children run into problems, don't criticize but help them focus and redefine based on their actual resources, time, and ability. Offer some solutions to get them back on their feet.

Like adults, many kids overextend themselves in their initial enthusiasm for a new enterprise.

Since children do not yet have a lot of experience with themselves, it's common for them to find they are stuck working at something they don't enjoy. At various short intervals, check with your children. Ask them if they are enjoying their business and what aspects of it they like or don't like. Help them use the insights to start something new that is more consistent with their personalities. Don't criticize but help make the change a learning experience.

Jobs for Kids

The best way for your children to decide what kind of job or work or business to do is to find something they like that matches their personality and interests. A shy or quiet child who works well alone probably wouldn't enjoy being a salesperson. And an outgoing, fun loving child will probably be miserable weeding gardens alone. Get your child to make a list of things they like to do, that they already do, and a list of things that interest them, and help them connect their likes and dislikes with different jobs and work styles. Start brainstorming work that uses the items on the list.

If your child spends lots of time on the computer, enjoys the technical side, and likes one-on-one relating to people, she might think of being a computer tutor. If he's athletic and good at sports, he might consider giving sports lessons, one-on-one, to younger kids. Check with the local recreation center or league directors of the sports he's interested in. If your child is academically oriented and does well in school, she can be a private tutor for other children. Talk with the schools and teachers about opportunities. A business card may help.

The best way for your children to decide what kind of job or work or business to do is to find something they like that matches their personality and interests.

The per-week gross income of 12 to 15-
year-olds was $25; of 16 and 17-year-
olds, $57; and of 18 and 19-year-olds,
$123.

Baby-sitting: Your child needs to let people know
that he sits and that he is looking for more sitting
jobs. He needs to let other parents know he's available. He might volunteer to help at the church nurs-
ery. It's a great way to meet parents with kids. Make
sure his name is in the neighborhood directory. He
can buy blank business cards at an office supply
store and print them up on the computer.

Here is a short list of typical jobs that are easy
for children to find and do:

Computer data entry
Computer/software teacher
Dog walking
Envelope stuffing and addressing
Errands and chores for the elderly
Filing
Flyer distributor
Garbage can mover
Gardening/weeding
Golf club caddie
Grocery delivery
Helping with parents' work
House cleaning
House sitting
Leaf raking
Organizing games for parties
Packing for a move
Painting (fences, garage, etc.)

Playing music for parties
Price shopper
Recycler
Salesperson
Snow shoveling
Sorting and organizing
Storage
Taking coats, serving snacks at parties
Videographer/Photographer
Wake-up caller
Window washer
Word processor
Yard sale
Yard work

Resources

Books

The Barron's Biz Kids' Guide To Success, by Terri Thompson (Barrons, 1992).

Better Than A Lemonade Stand, by Daryl Bernstein (Beyond Words Publishing, 1992).

Capitalism For Kids: Growing Up To Be Your Own Boss, by Karl Hess (Dearborn Financial, 1992).

The Career Coach, by Carol Kleiman (Berkley, 1995).

Fast Cash For Kids, by Bonnie and Noel Drew (Career Press, 1995).

Find The Career That Fits You, by Lee Ellis and Larry Burkett (Moody Press, 1993).

Lifetime Employability: How To Become Indispensible, by Carole Hyatt (Master Media, Ltd., 1996). Order by phone: 1-800-334-8232.

The Pathfinder: A Guide To Career Decision Making, by Lee Ellis (CFC). Order by phone: 1-800-722-1976.

The Teen's Guide To Business: The Secrets To A Successful Enterprise, by Linda Menzies, Oren S. Jenkins, and Rickell R. Fisher (Thorndike Press, 1993).

The Teenage Entrepreneur's Guide: 50 Money-Making Business Ideas, by Sarah Riehm (Surrey Books, 1987).

The Totally Awesome Business Book for Kids, by Adriane G. Berg (Newmarket, 1994).

Your Career In Changing Times, by Lee Ellis and Larry Burkett (Moody Press, 1993).

Pamphlets/Brochures

Business tips for pre-teens and up
Center for Entrepreneurship
Wichita State University
Wichita, KS 67208

The Handy Reference Guide to the Fair Labor Standards Act
U.S. Dept. of Labor
202-209-4907

"How to Prepare a Business Plan"
Young Americans Bank
311 Steele St.
Denver, CO 80206
303-321-2265

Videos

Teenage Entrepreneurs (vol. 25 of *That Teen Show*)
Saturn Productions, 1985

Internet

Businesses Your Child Can Run
http://www.elibrary.com/intuit/10005/fetcfh/kids_10
.htm

The Kidz Biz Invention Connection
on AOL at keyword: KIDZBIZ

Software

The Whatsit Corporation (ages 11 and up)
Apple II series, Commodore 64 (51/4" disk), IBM-
PC, PC Jr.
Wings for Learning-Sunburst
Scott's Valley, CA
1-800-321-7511

Kits

Kids Busines$
(A kit for budding entrepreneurs ages 10-18 to start
and run a business, $49.95)
1-800-282-KIDSW

Telephone Information

The Center for Entrepreneurship
(Resources and educational opportunities for future
entrepreneurs)
Wichita State University
1845 North Fairmount
Wichita, KS 68260
316-689-3000

Future Business Leaders of America (high school)
703-860-3334

Internal Revenue Service
1-800-829-3676

Junior Achievement (JA) — business basics for 5th
grade and up
5 Landmark Square
Stamford, CT 06901
203-327-2535

Social Security information
1-800-772-1213

U.S. Dept. of Labor
202-209-4907.

Programs

Chamber of Commerce (contact your local branch)

Learn to Earn
National 4-H Council
7100 Connecticut Ave.
Chevy Chase, MD 20815

The National Council on Economic Education
(State programs for kids to learn about business)
1140 Avenue of the Americas
New York, NY 10036
212-730-7007

Chapter 15

Children Of The Future

While teaching your kids money management principles and techniques, you need to be preparing financially for their future as well. There are a number of options for parents in all tax brackets to ensure their kids' financial security and protection. This chapter explains some of the financial and legal issues you will encounter and have to make decisions about when preparing for the future.

These are options only. I am not recommending any particular one or ones. I strongly advise that you check with an attorney or financial planner or investment advisor before making any decisions.

Custodial and Joint
Accounts for Minors

A lot of parents ask, "Should I hold investments in my child's name in a custodial account, or in a joint account held by me and my child?"

When investing for a minor child, it is usually not possible or desirable to make investments directly in the child's name. Most investments are made by an adult for a child through either a trust or custodial arrangement. Trust arrangements are often complex and can require a lengthy legal document, but custodial arrangements are relatively simple to establish under a special state law that is derived from one of two legal forms, referred to as either the Uniform Gifts to Minors Act (UGMA) or the Uniform Transfers to Minors Act (UTMA). While every state has either UGMA or UTMA, the laws in each state vary slightly.

Under typical laws it's easy to set up a custodial account for your child. A custodial account is basically a trust; you're putting the money in the child's name while you maintain the authority and authorization to manage that money for the child. The problem with that is that once children turn 18 or 21, depending on the state, its their money for them to do whatever they want. At that time, they can choose to spend it, and if they decide they want to spend it going camel riding in Africa instead of going to college or investing in a business, that's up to them, so you lose a little control eventually when you do a custodial account.

On the other hand, if you want to retain more control, you can set up a parent or guardian joint account with the child. That way you create a situation in which the child does not automatically get the money at some pre-ordained time. You may want to

A custodial account is basically a trust; you're putting the money in the child's name while you maintain the authority and authorization to manage that money for the child.

even consider holding the money in your own name, not put it in the child's name, but put it in a special account that you designate as being for the child. The only drawback is that you have to pay income taxes on the growth and capital gains on it at the adult tax rates. With a custodial account, the taxes are bypassed, or passed along to the child, who is usually in a lower tax bracket than the adult. But seek legal advice to find out what is best in your family and for your situation, and then do what's right for your family.

With a custodial account, the taxes are bypassed, or passed along to the child, who is usually in a lower tax bracket than the adult.

Legally, minors can't open an account in their own name. The rules vary by state, but essentially, minors can't have a banking or investment account without having a custodian account. This brings up the next big question, "Do I leave the money in my name with my child jointly? Or do I set up a separate Uniform Trust to Minors account?"

Most banks and mutual fund companies will try to get you to set up an UTMA. When you open an account for your child, you have to check a box for either an UTMA or a joint account. And people are confused by that. But deciding between them is really very simple.

You can set up a joint account with your name and your child's for bank accounts, real estate, stocks, and US bonds. Money in a joint account goes directly to the control of your child if you die. Joint accounts are not subject to probate, but generally they do not save taxes as the estate tax is attributed to the Social Security number on the account. In a joint account you always can control that money no matter how old that child is, and you can decide some day later to take it away from him.

If you want your child to maintain a sense of autonomy and control over the account, you can set up a joint account but not have your name printed on any of the deposit or withdrawal forms. Even though you, as the parent, have control, your child's perception is that the account is hers because hers is the only name that appears on the documents. There was no reminder that you have ultimate control and signing power.

An UGMA/UTMA custodian manages the assets held in the custodial account for the minor child until he or she is entitled to manage the assets, sometime between the ages of 18 and 21, depending on the state. The custodian is most often the child's parent or other adult member of the child's family. Only one person may be appointed to act as custodian at one time, but successors may be designated if the primary custodian becomes unavailable.

The assets held in an UGMA/UTMA custodial account become the child's property on attaining majority, and must be held for the child's exclusive benefit. This may include such things as a college education, the purchase of a new bike or car, or a vacation. The assets cannot be used for items that reflect parental obligations such as food, rent or clothing for the child, and the assets may not be used to personally benefit the custodian.

The assets in the account can be the child's own money or money that is a gift to the child, but any gifts made to the account are irrevocable. The child can request money from the account, but as long as the child is a minor, it is at the discretion of the custodian whether to grant the request.

Although all investment income paid to a custodial account is the property of the child, the taxation of that income depends on the child's age and the total income earned. (See following section on taxes.)

When the child reaches the legal age specified by the applicable state law, the custodian is required to turn over the assets to the child. This involves the

> The assets held in an UGMA/ UTMA custodial account become the child's property on attaining majority, and must be held for the child's exclusive benefit.

custodian instructing the investment company to re-register the account in the child's name alone.

In an UTMA, the account is in the child's name but you're responsible for managing it. When children reach majority, the account becomes their asset and is under their control. You lose control so you have to decide, when your child turns 18 or 21, whatever the state says, do you really want them to have responsibility for and control of the money or do you want to maintain control? Until majority, your children can't control it, but they own it. And when they turn 21 they can then control it, too.

A Custodial Account/Uniform Gift to Minors Act (UGMA) Account: offers parents tax advantages by allowing them to shift income to the child at a lower tax rate. Custodial accounts can be part of a gifting program used effectively in estate planning. Check with your tax advisor for details.

A client of mine wanted to give his twin granddaughters $150,000 each. The girls were minors so I managed the accounts for them but the grandfather maintained control and he directed how to invest it, using my guidance. When the grandfather died, the father took over control of the accounts as guardian for his daughters who were then 16. As soon as the father took over control, he came into my office.

"Mike, I need to take $10,000 out of each one of those accounts now."

I said, "Well, I can't do that because they're trust accounts and we don't issue cash. I can give you a check made out to you and both your daughters, but I can't give you cash."

He said, "Okay, do that." And that's what he did every week for about six weeks. His withdrawals totaled over $100,000.

I finally went to my manager and said, "This is weird. This guy's gotta be stealing this money."

A Custodial Account/Uniform Gift to Minors Act (UGMA) Account offers parents tax advantages by allowing them to shift income to the child at a lower tax rate.

The manager answered, "There's nothing you can do about it. He's the custodian of the accounts. The father was cashing the checks at the bank and blowing it on drugs. He didn't need his daughters' endorsement on the checks because they were minors. It turned out that the father was a drug addict and squandered most of the money left to his daughters. Basically these girls turned out with nothing. It was his option because he was the custodian. If you need to appoint a custodian of your estate, make sure it's somebody responsible.

Taxes on Minors

There are special tax rates which apply to children. The first $650 of investment income (and any other unearned income) from all sources in a single year is tax-free from federal income tax for children under 14. The next $650 is taxed at the minor's marginal tax rate of 15%, and any income over $1,300 is taxed at the marginal rate for income over $1,300 of the child's parents. This Kiddy Tax is to prevent parents from hiding their own money from taxation in custodial accounts for their kids. For children age 14 until they become independent or turn 21, all unearned income above $650 is taxed at the child's 15% marginal rate.

Wills

Only one third of the adults in this country have a will, which probably means that you're among the two-thirds that don't. Consider that, if something happens to you, your kids will face both legal and financial problems, possibly for years, while dealing with the emotional impact of your death. Be willing to discuss and explain your arrangements with your older children. Your wishes will matter to them and they need to know that you have provided for them.

Despite her enormous income from making films, Marilyn Monroe had virtually no money when she died. And Elvis Presley's estate executor had to start running tours through Graceland to pay his taxes.

You have a will whether you've prepared one or not. State laws provide a default will for anyone who dies intestate. The provisions may include:

- Probate Court appoints the executor;
- Half of all property goes to spouse, other half split among children;
- Surviving spouse is automatically children's guardian;
- A guardian is appointed by Probate Court if spouse dies;
- Surviving spouse has to make written account to Probate Court on how and why money is spent for children;
- Surviving spouse has to have a performance bond with sureties approved by Probate Court to guarantee they will handle children's money properly;

- When children become adults, surviving spouse
  has to file an itemized account of every expenditure of children's money over the years;
- Children take control of their share of estate at
  age 18;
- If spouse remarries, next spouse receives one
  third of surviving spouse's property to dispose
  of any way they want;
- Next spouse has no obligation to support your
  children;
- Death taxes are higher.

If these provisions don't reflect your preferences
for your family, you need to specify other arrangements in your own document. If you're financial circumstances aren't too complex and you don't want
to hire an attorney to help you draw up a will, there
is will-making computer software available and self-
help books.

Life Insurance

In addition to a will, life insurance is very important
to your children's financial security and protection.
It replaces income if you die; it affords the services
you provide as a housekeeper if you die; it provides
money to repay business loans or keep a business
going; it provides immediate cash for funeral and
burial expenses and estate taxes.

A good rule to follow when buying life insurance is to get a policy that's worth seven times your
current annual income. If you have large assets, you
may want to set up an irrevocable trust that will keep
the insurance proceeds out of your estate. (See section below on trusts.)

A good
rule to follow
when buying
life insurance
is to get a
policy that's
worth seven
times your
current annu-
al income.

If you want your kids to go to college, you may want to invest in more than term life insurance by finding insurance that includes some sort of savings or investments. You can cancel that part of the policy once your kids are on their own.

Insurance premiums are determined by age, gender, state of health when you first purchase it, and whether or not you smoke.

Whole Life:
This is a life insurance policy that includes a savings account.

Whole Life

This is a life insurance policy that includes a savings account. The savings accumulate as long as you pay for the policy. The estimated amount that will be saved varies over the years as the interest rates vary. There are no guarantees. There can be fees and charges for the death benefit that are deducted from your cash value before any interest is paid.

Term

Term:
You buy a policy for a set payment and pay annual premiums that usually increase slightly every year.

You buy a policy for a set payment and pay annual premiums that usually increase slightly every year. You can also get level term insurance which fixes the premium for a number of years before it jumps. The insurance is in force as long as you pay premiums. Term life is usually guaranteed renewable; you don't have to ever requalify with a medical exam. If you buy term insurance, you can invest the savings part in another savings investment of your choice at better interest and with less risk than with Whole Life.

Universal Life

This is the most flexible and also the riskiest because it is possible to lose all the money you invest in the savings part of the policy. You can get a guaranteed death benefit payment; you can accumulate tax-deferred savings; you can pay extra annual premiums to build up more saved cash.

What to look for in a life insurance policy:

- Non cancelable as long as you pay premiums;
- Guaranteed annual premium price;
- Waiver of premium payment while you are disabled;
- Residual benefit disability payment that pays you the difference between your full benefit and what you are able to earn after you are disabled.

It's a good idea to always have three to six months living expenses in your savings account. If you do, you can buy the 90 day start date on disability benefits and save a lot on premiums.

Universal Life: This is the most flexible and also the riskiest because it is possible to lose all the money you invest in the savings part of the policy.

Social Security

There are social security benefits available for unmarried dependent children under 18 and under 19 if they are still in secondary school.

Disability Insurance

Disability insurance pays benefits when you are permanently or temporarily:

- Totally incapacitated and confined to bed;

- Unable to work at any occupation;
- Unable to work at a specific occupation.

Premiums are based on how soon benefits start paying after you are disabled. On average, people who are temporarily disabled go back to work 21 days after an accident or illness.

Trusts

Trust funds are accounts that allow you to invest for and pass assets on to your children without disruption both during your lifetime and after your death. Once established, they exist as legal entities independent of your situation.

"Put not your trust in money, but put your money in trust."

— Oliver Wendell Holmes

There are two types of trusts, a living trust and a testamentary trust which you create in your will and which comes into being on your death. A testamentary trust controls your assets for the benefit of your beneficiary after your death. This is especially useful if your heir is a minor child or a young adult who is not yet financially responsible.

A living trust, also called an Inter Vivos Trust, is a legal entity that, like a person or company, can own, buy, and sell assets. There are two types of living trusts: revocable and irrevocable. With a revocable living trust, you can transfer some of your assets into the trust which you control and which you can change or revoke when you want. As long as you don't revoke it and do name a successor to manage it, the trust continues to perform on behalf of the beneficiary, uninterrupted, if you die or are incapacitated.

Once an asset is transferred to a trust, the asset is no longer considered part of the estate of the person establishing the trust. With a revocable trust, which you control, any income in the trust is your tax responsibility. With an irrevocable trust, the trust itself is taxed independently, but at a higher rate than individuals are taxed. If any of the income from a trust is distributed to the beneficiary, that distribution is taxed at the beneficiary's tax rate and is his or her responsibility.

Some of the advantages of trusts include:

- Saving estate taxes and protecting assets from creditors;
- Allowing for continuity of your financial and business concerns if you die or are incapacitated;
- Unlike a will, a trust is not a public document; there is complete privacy; only family and attorney know what's in it;
- You can name a trustee of your choice to manage the trust after you die;
- Assets in a trust are not subject to probate or the costs of probating a will;
- A trust can hold and manage assets for your children until they're grown;
- A trust reduces estate taxes on estates worth over $600,000;
- A trust can manage money left to a spouse;
- A trust can provide for disabled children.

Setting up a living trust through an estate attorney costs about $500 to $2,500 depending on attorney fees and on what you want to accomplish with the trust.

Family Business Partnerships

If you are a business owner, you can set up a Family Limited Partnership (FLP). One family member is named as the general partner who has the power to run the business, trade stock, sell real estate, or manage any other assets. Other family members are listed as limited partners who can't vote but who actually own most of the assets and who can receive rental or lease income from your business. The FLP can take the place of a trust in situations where estate planning and creditor protection are goals. FLPs allow you to:

- Transfer assets to children while you maintain control;
- Transfer your business to your children on your death without complications;
- Reduce taxes on the transferred assets;
- Saves estate taxes;
- Avoid cost of trustees;
- Protect assets against creditors.

Investing for College and Retirement

Two of the biggest savings challenges you have to deal with are your children's college tuition and your retirement. Both are important and you don't want to favor one to the detriment of the other.

In order to find the right savings balance for yourself, you need to analyze your current financial status along with your time horizon for each investment objective and tolerance for risk. By analyzing your current situation, you should be able to determine how much you can comfortably put aside for college and retirement, whether on a monthly or quarterly basis. You can also consult with a financial advisor. Their expertise and guidance can be of help in designing and implementing an investment plan that will help you achieve your desired goals.

To help balance parents' retirement savings with kid's college savings, consider taking advantage of your employer's 401(k) or 403(b) plans; or if you're self employed, a retirement account like a Keogh. Additionally, you may want to consider an individual retirement account (IRA).   These retirement accounts offer two advantages over taxable investment accounts: your contributions grow on a tax-deferred basis and the contributions may reduce your current income tax bill.

"The earlier you start saving, the less money you'll have to sock away overall —

your savings will appreciate through investments . . . . Take advantage of the varying tax rates by shifting funds to your children. Up to age 14, your children get a tax advantage on investment earnings of up to $1,300 a year and on

earned income of up to $28,000 a year.
The $1,300 yearly, if reinvested well,
might grow to $50,000 or so by the time
college rolls around."

— Jill Andresky Fraser
(Inc. magazine finance editor)

Finding Professional
Financial Planning Help

To write a will or set up a trust fund, you need an attorney who specializes in Wills, Trusts, and Estate Planning. Ask your lawyer or friends you trust to refer you or call the Bar Association in your state for a list of qualified names.

For your investments, you probably want to work with a financial planner. If you have a significant portfolio, you probably need to see one on a regular basis. If your income and portfolio are average, an occasional visit for fine-tuning will do. Never make a recommended investment until you understand exactly what the potential risks and benefits are.

There are several things to keep in mind when seeking an appropriate financial planner for your situation. There is no state or federal regulation of financial planners and no exam they have to pass so their qualifications vary enormously. Some consultants advertise themselves as planners when they're not.

Interview several candidates for comfort as you will be sharing personal information about all your money matters, divorce, losses and gains, children and heirs with your planner. When interviewing a potential financial planner, the first step is to ask whether the planner is a member of one of three well-regarded national professional associations: the Institute of Certified Financial Planners, the International Association for Financial Planning, or the National Association of Personal Financial Advisors (NAPFA). Ask about qualifications and training and check with the Better Business Bureau. Some planners are paid on a commission basis and are affiliated with insurance companies or broker-ages and are paid a commission when they sign you up for a policy or investment. Ask if they are selling only financial products from firms they represent or if they sell a variety of products from different com-panies. Fee-only planners, such as those affiliated with NAPFA, do not work on a commission basis. Their only compensation is the fees from clients for their recommendations. They do not receive com-missions from companies whose products they are trying to sell.

"Nothing is cheap which is superfluous, for what one does not need, is dear at a penny."

— Plutarch

Registered investment advisors who make specific investment recommendations, must be registered with the federal Securities and Exchange

Commission (SEC) and file a form called an ADV. Ask to see the planner's ADV, Part Two. It recounts their experience, investment strategies, conflicts of interest, and fee structure.

Planner Designations

CMFC: Chartered Mutual Fund Counselor. These planners have passed an exam covering their knowledge of mutual funds and have agreed to a code of ethics. They are certified by the National Endowment for Financial Education with the Investment Company Institute.

CFP: Certified Financial Planner. These planners have been licensed by the CFP Board of Standards. They have passed a comprehensive exam, have one to five years financial services experience, adhere to a code of ethics, and are required to fulfill continuing education course requirements.

CFA: Chartered Financial Analyst. These planners have passed an exam on investments and finance and are certified by the Financial Analysts Federation.

PFS: Personal Financial Specialist. These planners are certified public accountants who also have several years of financial planning experience.

Planner Organizations

ICFP: The Institute of Certified Financial Planners. Members hold, or are working towards, a certified financial planner license.

IAFP: The International Association for Financial Planning. There are four membership categories: general members include anyone in financial services, brokers or practitioners licensed in either securities, insurance, or as investment advisors.

NAPFA: The National Association of Personal Financial Advisers. Registered investment advisers who are fee-only planners.

Preparing financially for the future provides you with reassurance about your family and long-term security for children.

Resources

Internet

American Association of Individual Investors
http://networth.galt.com/www/home/planning/aaii/refer/selbrokr.html

Association for Special Kids-Money Matters
"Funding a Special Needs Trust with Survivorship Life Insurance," By Dr. Nita Savader, Chartered Financial Consultant, A.S.K.
http://www.specialkids.com/article.html

Books

Taking the Bite Out Of Insurance: How To Save Money On Life Insurance (NICO, 1997).

Nolo's Simple Will Book, by Denis Clifford (Nolo Press, 1995).

Information

Social Security
(you can check adult and kids benefits anytime with form SSA-7004, the Personal Earnings Benefit Estimate Statement (PEBES))
1-800-234-5772

NICO (National Insurance Consumer Organization)
(provides maximum rates, updated annually, consumers should pay for annual renewable term life insurance)
121 N. Payne St.
Alexandria, VA 22314

Weiss Research
(rating of insurance company safety, $15)
1-800-289-9222

Insurance Information

For $50, organization will send you names and
phone numbers of five insurance companies that
offer lowest term rates, guaranteed at least $50 less
premium than you currently pay for your situation.
1-800-472-5800

Life Insurance Advisors' Association (LIAA)
(fee only, low cost, non-commissioned insurance and
policy review)
1-800-521-4578

USAA
(sells disability insurance directly to the consumer
without an agent)
San Antonio, TX
1-800-531-8000

Insurance Price-Quote Services

TermQuote
Dayton, OH
1-800-444-8376

SelectQuote
San Francisco, CA
1-800-343-1985

InsuranceQuote
Chandler, AZ
1-800-972-1104

Finding A Financial Planner

The Institute of Certified Financial Planners
(For a list of certified planners in your area)
1-800-282-PLAN

The International Association for Financial Planning
(provides up to 5 names of financial planners in your
area, a brochure, and a financial planner disclosure
form)
1-800-945-IAFP

The National Association of Personal Financial
Advisors
(provides a list of fee-onlu planners in your area and
information about financial planners)
1-888- FEE-ONLY

Family Limited Partnerships

Adriane G. Berg, attorney
c/o Friedland, Fishbein, Laifer & Robbins
233 Broadway
New York, NY 10279
(212) 962-4888

Index

Mail/Fax Order Form

Summit Financial Publishing
19590 E. Main St., ste. 108
Parker, CO 80134

Toll-Free 24-hour Ordering and
Customer Service
Phone: 1.800.367.2548
Fax: 1.888.694-0318

ORDERED BY:	SHIP TO:
Name_____	Name_____
Address_____	Address_____
City, State, Zip _____	City, State, Zip _____

Phone _____
  Day _____
	Phone _____
	  Day _____

ITEMS ORDERED:

Item	Quantity	Unit Price	Total
Book			
Tape			
Total Price of Items			
Colorado Residents Add 6.8% Sales Tax			
Add $2 Per Book or Tape for Shipping and Handling			
TOTAL			

METHOD OF PAYMENT:

❑ Check Enclosed (Please make checks payable to World of Money
❑ Visa   ❑ MasterCard   ❑ AMEX   ❑ Discover

Account Number _____

Expiration Date _____

Customer Signature _____

"AS IS" LICENSE AGREEMENT AND LIMITED WARRANTY

READ THIS LICENSE CAREFULLY BEFORE OPENING THIS PACKAGE. BY OPENING THIS PACKAGE, YOU ARE AGREEING TO THE TERMS AND CONDITIONS OF THIS LICENSE. IF YOU DO NOT AGREE, DO NOT OPEN THE PACKAGE. PROMPTLY RETURN THE UNOPENED PACKAGE AND ALL ACCOMPANYING ITEMS TO THE PLACE YOU OBTAINED THEM. *THESE TERMS APPLY TO ALL LICENSED SOFTWARE ON THE DISK EXCEPT THAT THE TERMS FOR USE OF ANY SHAREWARE OR FREEWARE ON THE DISKETTES ARE AS SET FORTH IN THE ELECTRONIC LICENSE LOCATED ON THE DISK:*

1. GRANT OF LICENSE and OWNERSHIP: The enclosed computer programs ("Software") are licensed, not sold, to you by Pearson Education Canada Inc. ("We" or the "Company") in consideration of your adoption of the accompanying Company textbooks and/or other materials, and your agreement to these terms. You own only the disk(s) but we and/or our licensors own the Software itself. This license allows instructors and students enrolled in the course using the Company textbook that accompanies this Software (the "Course") to use and display the enclosed copy of the Software for academic use only, so long as you comply with the terms of this Agreement. You may make one copy for back up only. We reserve any rights not granted to you.

2. USE RESTRICTIONS: You may <u>not</u> sell or license copies of the Software or the Documentation to others. You may <u>not</u> transfer, distribute or make available the Software or the Documentation, except to instructors and students in your school who are users of the adopted Company textbook that accompanies this Software in connection with the course for which the textbook was adopted. You may <u>not</u> reverse engineer, disassemble, decompile, modify, adapt, translate or create derivative works based on the Software or the Documentation. You may be held legally responsible for any copying or copyright infringement which is caused by your failure to abide by the terms of these restrictions.

3. TERMINATION: This license is effective until terminated. This license will terminate automatically without notice from the Company if you fail to comply with any provisions or limitations of this license. Upon termination, you shall destroy the Documentation and all copies of the Software. All provisions of this Agreement as to limitation and disclaimer of warranties, limitation of liability, remedies or damages, and our ownership rights shall survive termination.

4. DISCLAIMER OF WARRANTY: THE COMPANY AND ITS LICENSORS MAKE <u>NO</u> WARRANTIES ABOUT THE SOFTWARE, WHICH IS PROVIDED "<u>AS-IS</u>." IF THE DISK IS DEFECTIVE IN MATERIALS OR WORKMANSHIP, YOUR ONLY REMEDY IS TO RETURN IT TO THE COMPANY WITHIN 30 DAYS FOR REPLACEMENT UNLESS THE COMPANY DETERMINES IN GOOD FAITH THAT THE DISK HAS BEEN MISUSED OR IMPROPERLY INSTALLED, REPAIRED, ALTERED OR DAMAGED. THE COMPANY DISCLAIMS ALL WARRANTIES, EXPRESS OR IMPLIED, INCLUDING WITHOUT LIMITATION, THE IMPLIED WARRANTIES OF MERCHANTABILITY AND FITNESS FOR A PARTICULAR PURPOSE. THE COMPANY DOES NOT WARRANT, GUARANTEE OR MAKE ANY REPRESENTATION REGARDING THE ACCURACY, RELIABILITY, CURRENTNESS, USE, OR RESULTS OF USE, OF THE SOFTWARE.

5. LIMITATION OF REMEDIES AND DAMAGES: IN NO EVENT, SHALL THE COMPANY OR ITS EMPLOYEES, AGENTS, LICENSORS OR CONTRACTORS BE LIABLE FOR ANY INCIDENTAL, INDIRECT, SPECIAL OR CONSEQUENTIAL DAMAGES ARISING OUT OF OR IN CONNECTION WITH THIS LICENSE OR THE SOFTWARE, INCLUDING, WITHOUT LIMITATION, LOSS OF USE, LOSS OF DATA, LOSS OF INCOME OR PROFIT, OR OTHER LOSSES SUSTAINED AS A RESULT OF INJURY TO ANY PERSON, OR LOSS OF OR DAMAGE TO PROPERTY, OR CLAIMS OF THIRD PARTIES, EVEN IF THE COMPANY OR AN AUTHORIZED REPRESENTATIVE OF THE COMPANY HAS BEEN ADVISED OF THE POSSIBILITY OF SUCH DAMAGES. SOME JURISDICTIONS DO NOT ALLOW THE LIMITATION OF DAMAGES IN CERTAIN CIRCUMSTANCES, SO THE ABOVE LIMITATIONS MAY NOT ALWAYS APPLY.

6. GENERAL: THIS AGREEMENT SHALL BE CONSTRUED AND INTERPRETED ACCORDING TO THE LAWS OF THE PROVINCE OF ONTARIO. This Agreement is the complete and exclusive statement of the agreement between you and the Company and supersedes all proposals, prior agreements, oral or written, and any other communications between you and the company or any of its representatives relating to the subject matter.

Should you have any questions concerning this agreement or if you wish to contact the Company for any reason, please contact in writing: Editorial Manager, Pearson Education Canada, 26 Prince Andrew Place, Don Mills, Ontario, M3C 2T8.

Interactive Figures and Maps

HandsOnSociology, Macionis Edition features interactive versions of some of the figures and maps found in your textbook. These figures and maps are organized by topic. To open a figure or map, simply click on its title. Rolling your mouse over any of the items in the legend will highlight the relevant countries in the world. Clicking on a legend item will fix the pertinent countries on the map, and will allow you to compare them with other sets of countries.

Flashcards

HandsOnSociology, Macionis Edition offers sets of interactive flashcards to help you remember the key term definitions from your text. Click on the link to see the flashcards from your text. The flashcards are organized by chapter. Click on a card to bring up a term from the chapter, and then click on the card again to see the definition.

Recommended System and Software Requirements

Hardware Requirements

IBM Compatible
Pentium 133 MHz
64 MB RAM
20 MB hard drive space

Soundcard and speakers
SVGA monitor displaying 256 or
more colours
4X or faster CD-ROM
Mouse

Software Requirements

Javascript Enabled Web Browser —
Internet Explorer 5.5 (or higher) or
Netscape 6.0.2 (or higher)
recommended.

Macromedia Shockwave Player (version
8.5.1 included on CD).

*Note: This product may run on computers that don't
meet the recommended requirements, but performance may be slow or unstable.

Animated Sociology Tutorials

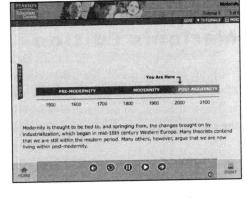

HandsOnSociology, Macionis Edition includes 15 animated sociology tutorials. Each of these tutorials explores one of the core topics in introductory sociology using animation and an accompanying audio lecture. Each tutorial also contains a quiz, links to relevant websites, and a glossary.

Clicking on the links from the Animated Sociology page will take you to the selected "Animated Tutorial" for that topic.

Navigating through a tutorial is easy. Five buttons at the bottom of each page allow you to: go back to the last page visited, replay the animation of the current page, pause the animation, play the animation, and go to the next page in the unit. Clicking on the speaker button allows you to turn on or off the audio lecture that accompanies each unit.

In the bottom corner on the left of your screen, you will see the title "Home," which takes you to the page listing all 15 modules. There are also three buttons at the top of each page. "Quiz" takes you to a set of questions tailored to each tutorial, which gives you the chance to reinforce your learning. "Tutorials" provides a link to the homepage of each tutorial, and "Index" provides a list of all pages in the current module.

The "More Info" button is usually available at the left side of the screen. When you click this button, a pull-down menu appears. Depending on the unit you are in, the menu choices will vary, but could include links, definitions, and other information related to the topic. Clicking any of those menu choices will open a text box containing the relevant information.

In the bottom corner on the right, you will see the word "Print" and a small printer icon. Click on this icon to print the screen that you are currently reading.

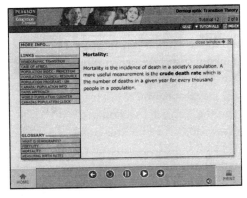

How to Use HandsOnSociology, Macionis Edition

There are four distinct components to HandsOnSociology—the 2001 Census: a profile of Canada's population, animated sociology tutorials, interactive figures and maps, and flashcards. Each of these components ties into your textbook, and will help you get the most value out of your learning experience.

The 2001 Census: A Profile of Canada's Population

This component includes information drawn from the most recent releases of census data by the Government of Canada. A variety of topic areas are covered: where we live, Canada ages, the diversification of families continues, the languages spoken in Canada, the ethnocultural portrait of Canada and the Aboriginal population, Canadians at work, earnings of Canadians, analyzing family income, education of Canadians, and religion in Canada.

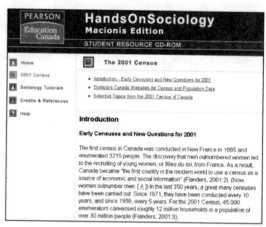

The content within each topic area is directly correlated with specific chapters and pages of your textbook. The "Highlights" section provides an in-depth investigation of the census material. Wherever you see a map or a table indicated, you can click on that link and see the Statistics Canada information being referred to. The "Critical Thinking" section presents several questions that encourage you to think more deeply about the information you've just read, and the "Projects" section proposes a topic for a research project that could be done by an individual or by a group.

An Introduction to HandsOnSociology, Macionis Edition

Welcome to HandsOnSociology, Macionis Edition, Pearson Education Canada's innovative learning tool designed to accompany the latest Canadian editions of *Sociology* and *Society: The Basics*. Whether you are looking to solidify your understanding of core topics, or looking to apply your critical thinking skills to real-life sociological topics, this special edition of HandsOnSociology is for you.

HandsOnSociology, Macionis Edition Contents

The 2001 Census: A Profile of Canada's Population
>   Where We Live
>   Canada Ages
>   The Diversification of Families Continues
>   The Languages Spoken in Canada
>   The Ethnocultural Portrait of Canada and the Aboriginal Population
>   Canadians at Work
>   Earnings of Canadians
>   Analyzing Family Income
>   Education of Canadians
>   Religion in Canada

Animated Sociology Tutorials
>   Norms
>   Race and Ethnicity: Patterns of Interaction
>   Capitalism and Socialism
>   Global Stratification: Correlates of Poverty
>   Types of Social Movements
>   Divorce: Canadian Style
>   Presentation of Self
>   Modernity
>   Malthusian Theory
>   Bureaucracies
>   The Protestant Work Ethic
>   Demographic Transition Theory
>   Education and Functionalism
>   Methods of Sociological Research
>   Deviance: Symbolic Interactionist Perspectives

Interactive Figures and Maps
Flashcards

Contents

Welcome

Since it is very important to know the latest sociological data in order to provide up-to-date answers to the central questions of sociology, we have developed HandsOnSociology, Macionis Edition to present data from the ongoing releases of the 2001 Census of Canada in an easy-to-use interactive CD format. In this package are the highlights of the releases about where we live, our age-sex distribution, our families, our languages spoken, our ethnocultural mosaic, where we work, what we earn, our education, and our religious beliefs. Critical thinking questions are included for you to assess your understanding and consider the implications of the data, and a project is suggested to encourage you to work with the census data to develop a greater understanding of it and its place in a larger sociological portrait of society.

Edward G. Thompson

As part of our ongoing effort to find new and innovative ways to enhance the educational experience, Pearson Education Canada presents 15 instructional modules covering key concepts in sociology. By combining the communicative power of audio, universal symbols, movement, and text, the modules help you learn the key concepts quickly and accurately. Each module provides a clear explanation of the core issues, as well as complementary resources.

Knowledge eLearning